THE

COMPANIES ACT

1967

Some Requirements and Implications

ACCOUNTANTS' PUBLISHING CO. LTD. for

**The Institute of
Chartered Accountants of Scotland**

First Printed   *August 1967*
Reprinted   *September 1967*
Reprinted   *November 1967*

INTRODUCTION

THIS booklet is intended for accountants (both in and out of public practice) and those who have to do with the affairs of companies. The purpose of the booklet is to help them to understand the changes made in company law by the passing of the Companies Act 1967, on July 27, 1967, and to alert them to some of the problems arising from such changes. To achieve this the booklet deals with its subject in two ways—by a factual statement of the effect on company law of the requirements of the new Companies Act (Chapter I), and by an analysis by a number of authors of the problems which immediately occur to them as requiring consideration by interested parties (Chapters II to V). The opinions expressed in the latter chapters are those of the individual authors.

In view of indications that the Government intends introducing a series of Acts to amend company law no attempt has been made in this booklet to deal with points with which the Companies Act 1967 is not concerned. For example, the subject of no par value shares has been ignored. Moreover, because they are of interest only to a specialist readership, the new provisions relating to insurance companies, to banks and to shipping companies have been omitted from the present publication.

The booklet has been prepared at the request and under the supervision of a Sub-Committee drawn from the Company Law Committee and the Research and Publications Committee of The Institute of Chartered Accountants of Scotland. This Sub-Committee would like to express its gratitude to the authors who have provided the material for the booklet and to the secretariat of the Institute for its help in the preparation.

EDINBURGH, *25th August, 1967*

CONTENTS

CHAPTER II—REQUIREMENTS ON DISCLOSURE

CHAPTER IV—TAXATION AND ESTATE DUTY PROBLEMS ARISING ON CONSIDERATION OF THE COMPANIES ACT 1967

CHAPTER V—THE QUALIFICATIONS, APPOINTMENT, DUTIES AND RE-SPONSIBILITIES OF AUDITORS UNDER THE COMPANIES ACT 1967 *Page* 83

In chapters II to V references, unless otherwise stated, are to the Companies Act 1967. For references in chapter I, see paragraph 1 of that chapter.

CHAPTER I

COMPANY LAW AS AFFECTED BY THE COMPANIES ACT 1967

1. In this chapter factual information is given regarding the effects of the passing of the Companies Act 1967 upon company law as laid down in the Companies Act 1948 but no attempt is made to cover the special provisions which affect insurance companies, banks, shipping companies and moneylenders. The new Act reproduces many of the provisions of the earlier Act, and these are shown below in ordinary type: **the bold type indicates requirements and amendments introduced by the Companies Act 1967.** Paragraph references are to Schedule 2 of the 1967 Act and section references are to the 1967 Act unless otherwise indicated.

DISCLOSURE IN ACCOUNTS

2. Greater disclosure of information in the accounts of companies is required by the Companies Act 1967, and the following is a summary of what is required to be disclosed under the Companies Acts of 1948 and 1967. It will be appreciated that the details required have to be given unless, in some cases, their omission can be justified on the grounds of immateriality.

BALANCE SHEET

3. **SHARE CAPITAL**

   (1) Summary of authorised and issued share capital. Para. 2

   (2) Part of share capital consisting of redeemable preference shares and earliest and **latest date on which company has power to redeem those shares and whether those shares must be redeemed in any event or are liable to be redeemed at the option of the company and a note of the amount (if any) of the premium payable on redemption.** Para. 2(a)

   (3) Share capital on which interest has been paid out of capital during the financial year and rate of interest paid (so far as not given in the profit and loss account). Para. 2(b)

    (4) Particulars of any redeemed debentures which the company
has power to reissue.   Para. 2(d)

    (5) Number, description and amount of any shares in the
company which any person has an option to subscribe for,
together with period during which option is exercisable and
price to be paid for shares subscribed for under it.   Para.11(2)

4. RESERVES AND PROVISIONS

    (1) **It is not now necessary to distinguish between capital and
revenue reserves as was the case under the 1948 Act.**

    (2) Amount of share premium account and capital redemption
reserve fund.   1948 Act,
sec. 58
and
Para. 2(c)

    (3) Where the replacement of fixed assets is provided for wholly
or partly by charging cost of replacement against a provision
previously made for that purpose or by charging the cost
of replacement direct to revenue a note must be given of
the means by which the replacement is provided for and
the aggregate amount of the provision made but not used.   Para. 5(4)

    (4) **Aggregate amounts respectively of reserves and provisions.**   Para. 6

    (5) Sources of increases in and application of decreases in
reserves and provisions (unless shown in profit and loss
account).   Para. 7

5. LIABILITIES

    (1) **Amount set aside for the purpose of being used to prevent
undue fluctuations in charges for taxation and details where
used for another purpose.**   Para. 7A
and11(8A)

    (2) Aggregate of bank loans and overdrafts.   Para.
8(1)(d)

    (3) **Aggregate of other loans to the company which are not
wholly repayable within five years, showing terms of repayment and rate of interest in respect of each loan.**   Para.
8(1)(d)
and 8(4)

    (4) **Gross amount** recommended for distribution as dividend.   Para.
8(1)(e)

(5) Note of any liability of the company secured otherwise than by law on any assets of the company.   Para. 9

(6) Nominal amount of the company's debentures held by a nominee or trustee for the company, together with amount at which debentures are stated in company books.   Para. 10

(7) Amount of arrears of fixed cumulative dividends on company's shares and period for which dividends (of each class) are in arrear.   Para.11(3)

(8) General nature and amount of contingent liabilities not provided for.   Para.11(5)

(9) **Capital expenditure authorised by directors but not contracted for** and aggregate amount, or estimated amount, of contracts for capital expenditure (so far as not provided for).   Para. 11(6)

(10) **Basis of computation of amount set aside for United Kingdom corporation tax.**   Para. 11(10)

6. **ASSETS (EXCEPT INVESTMENTS)**

   (1) **Grouped under fixed, current and neither fixed nor current.**   Para. 4(2)

   (2) Method or methods used to arrive at amount of fixed assets under each heading.   Para. 4(3) and 5

   (3) Amount of goodwill, patents and trade marks (so far as not written off).   Para. 8(1)(b)

   (4) Aggregate of outstanding loans for purchase of company's own shares by employees.   Para. 8(1)(c)

   (5) Particulars of any charge on assets to secure the liabilities of any other person.   Para.11(4)

   (6) **If fixed assets shown at valuation—year of valuation and amount; and if valued during year under review—names or qualifications of valuers together with basis of valuation used.**   Para. 11(6A)

   (7) **Aggregate amount of fixed assets acquired during year and of assets disposed of or destroyed during year.**   Para. 11(6B)

(8) **Land to be subdivided amongst freehold, long (50 years or over) leasehold or short leasehold.**   Para. 11(6C)

(9) Whether, in the opinion of the directors, any of the current assets do not have a value at least equal to the amount at which they are stated.   Para.11(7)

(10) **Manner of computation of amount carried forward for stock in trade or work in progress.**   Para. 11(8B)

(11) Amount of loans made during the company's financial year to any officer of the company together with outstanding amounts of loans made to officers at any time before the company's financial year.   1948 Act, sec. 197

7. INVESTMENTS

(1) **For unquoted investments (other than any whose values as estimated by the directors are separately shown) where holding is in equity share capital of a company:—**

  (*a*) **aggregate of reporting company's income from the investments during year under review,**

  (*b*) **reporting company's share of the aggregate profits (less losses) before and after taxation,**

  (*c*) **accumulated share of the aggregate undistributed profits (less losses) of the companies, in which the investments are held, since the investments were acquired, and**

  (*d*) **manner in which any losses incurred by the companies in which the investments are held have been treated in the reporting company's accounts.**   Para. 5A

(2) **Aggregate amounts respectively of company's quoted and unquoted investments.**   Para. 8(1)(a) and 5(2)(c)

(3) Quoted investments to distinguish between those for which there has and those for which there has not been granted permission to deal on a recognised stock exchange.   Para. 8(3)

(4) **The aggregate market value of the company's quoted investments where it differs from the amount of the investments as stated, and the stock exchange value of any investments of which the market value is shown as being higher than the stock exchange value.**   Para.11(8)

(5) For holdings of any class of equity share capital of another body corporate (not being a subsidiary) exceeding in nominal value one-tenth of the nominal value of the issued capital of that class, disclose name of company in which shares held, where incorporated or registered, identity of class of shares held and proportion, together with like information regarding other classes of shares held in company. Similar information where investment amounts to at least one-tenth of assets of holding company (the Act specifies certain exemptions for companies incorporated or trading outside the U.K. if the Board of Trade agrees that disclosure could be harmful). Sec. 4

8. SUBSIDIARY COMPANIES (INCLUDING HOLDINGS THROUGH INTERMEDIATE SUBSIDIARIES)

(1) Holding company to disclose each subsidiary's name, specified details in relation to the country of incorporation, the class of shares held in the subsidiary and the proportion of the nominal value of the issued shares of the same class, distinguishing between subsidiary company shares held directly by the parent company and shares held in one subsidiary through another subsidiary. (The Act specifies certain exemptions for subsidiaries incorporated or trading outside the U.K. if the Board of Trade agrees that disclosure could be harmful.) Sec. 3

(2) Subsidiary to state the name of the company regarded by the directors as being the subsidiary company's ultimate holding company and the country of the holding company's incorporation.* Sec. 5

(3) Aggregate amount of assets consisting of shares in or amounts owing from subsidiaries and aggregate amount of indebtedness to subsidiaries. Para.15(2)

(4) Number, description and amount of shares in and debentures of the company held by its subsidiaries or their nominees. Para.15(3)

(5) Aggregate indebtedness to all companies of which reporting company is a subsidiary or fellow subsidiary, and the aggregate amount of indebtedness of all such bodies corporate to reporting company, distinguishing in each instance in respect of debentures and other indebtedness. Para.16(1)

* This information is not required in the case of a company trading overseas if the directors consider disclosure would be harmful and the Board of Trade agrees.

(6) **Aggregate amount of assets consisting of shares in fellow subsidiaries.**

Para. 16(1)

(7) Where group accounts are not submitted, there must be annexed to the balance sheet a statement showing:—

   (*a*) reasons why subsidiaries are not dealt with in group accounts,

   (*b*) net aggregate amount, so far as it concerns members of the holding company, of subsidiaries' profits less losses for respective financial years of the subsidiaries ending with or during the financial year of the company together with similar information for the previous financial years since they became the holding company's subsidiaries (distinguishing between amounts dealt with and those not dealt with in the company's accounts),

   (*c*) any material qualification contained in the report of the auditors of the subsidiaries on their accounts for the respective financial years of the subsidiaries.

Para.15(4)

(8) Where group accounts are not submitted and the financial years of the subsidiaries do not end with that of the holding company there must be annexed to the balance sheet a statement showing:—

   (*a*) reasons why company's directors consider that subsidiaries' financial years should not end with that of the company, and

   (*b*) the dates on which the subsidiaries' financial years ending last before that of the company respectively ended or the earliest and latest of those dates.

Para.15(6)

9. PRELIMINARY, ETC., EXPENSES

So far as not written off, separate headings for:—

preliminary expenses,
expenses in connection with issue of share capital or debentures,
commission in respect of shares or debentures,
discount allowed in respect of debentures,
discount allowed on issue of shares at a discount.

Para. 3

10. GENERAL

(1) Basis on which foreign currencies have been converted into sterling.   Para.11(9)

(2) Corresponding figures at end of immediately preceding financial year for all items.   Para. 11 (11) and sec. 10 and 11

PROFIT AND LOSS ACCOUNT

11. DIRECTORS' EMOLUMENTS

(1) Aggregate amount of directors' emoluments (including emoluments from subsidiary companies), distinguishing fees as directors, other emoluments, pensions and compensation for loss of office.   1948 Act, sec. 196

(2)*Emoluments of chairman (during period as chairman unless his duties as chairman were wholly or mainly discharged outside the U.K.).   Sec. 6(1)(a)

(3)*Number of directors in any of the following categories:—
  (a) receiving nil to £2,500 per annum,
  (b) receiving £2,500 per annum to £5,000 per annum— and so on in brackets of £2,500 per annum each time (unless their duties as directors were wholly or mainly discharged outside the U.K.).   Sec. 6(1)(b)

(4)*Emoluments of highest paid director where he is not also the chairman (unless his duties as director were wholly or mainly discharged outside the U.K.).   Sec. 6(2)

(5) Numbers of directors who have waived rights to receive emoluments and aggregate amount of emoluments so waived.   Sec. 7

12. INCOME

(1) Amount of income respectively from quoted and unquoted investments.   Para. 12(1)(g)

(2) Amount of net revenue of rents from land if substantial part of company's revenue.   Para. 12(1)(ga)

* For exemptions see paragraph 21. Emoluments for the purposes of paragraph 11(2)–(4) exclude contributions paid under any pension scheme (sec. 6(3)) but otherwise are as required to be disclosed under section 196 of the 1948 Act.

B

13. EXPENDITURE

(1) Amount of interest on bank loans, overdrafts, other loans repayable within five years whether by instalments or not and loans of other kinds.　　　Para. 12(1)(b)

(2) Amount charged to revenue in respect of the hire of plant and machinery.　　　Para. 12(1)(gb)

(3) Amount of remuneration of auditors (including expenses).　Para. 13

14. TURNOVER

*Turnover for year and method by which turnover is arrived at, note regarding omissions of turnover (if any).　　　Para. 13A

15. DEPRECIATION

(1) Amount charged to revenue by way of provision for depreciation, renewals or diminution in value of fixed assets.　　　Para. 12(1)(a)

(2) Amounts charged for provision for renewal of assets for which there has also been a depreciation charge.　　Para. 12(3)

(3) Where depreciation charge has not been determined by reference to value of assets shown in balance sheet this must be stated.　　Para. 12(4)

(4) Method of providing for depreciation, if other than by a depreciation charge or provision for renewals, or the fact that it is not provided for.　　Para. 14(2)

16. RESERVES and PROVISIONS

(1) Amounts respectively provided for redemption of share capital and for redemption of loans.　　Para. 12(1)(d)

(2) Amount set aside to or withdrawn from reserves.　　Para. 12(1)(e)

(3) Amount set aside to provisions (other than for depreciation, renewals or diminutions in value of assets) and amount withdrawn from such provisions and not applied for the purposes thereof.　　Para. 12(1)(f)

* For exemptions see paragraph 21.

17. TAXATION

(1) Amount of charge for U.K. corporation tax together with a note of the amount it would have been but for double taxation relief, the amount of charge for U.K. income tax and the amount of overseas taxation on profits, income and (so far as charged to revenue) capital gains.

Para. 12(1)(c)

(2) The basis on which the charge for **United Kingdom corporation tax** and United Kingdom income tax is computed.

Para. 14(3)

(3) Any special circumstances which affect liability in respect of taxation of profits, income or capital gains for the financial year or which will affect it in succeeding financial years.

Para. 14(3A)

18. DIVIDENDS

Aggregate amount (**before deduction of tax**) of the dividends paid and proposed.

Para. 12(1)(h)

19. SUNDRY

(1) Number of persons (except those wholly or mainly employed outside the U.K. and other than directors) whose emoluments are £10,000 a year or more—bracketed in groups rising by £2,500 a year each time. (Emoluments include those receivable from subsidiary companies and are as defined by sec. 196 of the 1948 Act except that contributions paid under pension schemes are excluded.)

Sec. 8

(2) Charges or credits arising in consequence of occurrences in a preceding financial year unless included in a heading relating to other matters.

Para. 12A

(3) Corresponding figures for immediately preceding financial year for all items.

Para. 14(5) and sec. 10 and 11

(4) Any material respects in which items in profit and loss account are affected by a change of the basis of accounting or by exceptional or non-recurrent transactions of a sort not usually undertaken by the company.

Para. 14(6)

GROUP ACCOUNTS

20. (1) The consolidated balance sheet and profit and loss account shall combine the information contained in the separate balance sheets and profit and loss accounts of the holding company and of the subsidiaries dealt with by the consolidated accounts, but with such adjustments (if any) as the directors of the holding company think necessary.   Para. 17

(2) The consolidated accounts must comply with the requirements of the Companies Acts of 1948 **and 1967** as if they were the accounts of an actual company.   Para. 18

(3) The following need not be shown in the consolidated accounts:—

(a) statement *re* **companies in which the reporting company is a shareholder but is not their holding company (sec. 4),**

and in respect of subsidiary company employees who are not also the reporting company's directors/employees:—

(b) particulars of directors' emoluments **including waivers** (1948 Act, sec. 196, **secs. 6-7**),

(c) particulars of loans to officers (1948 Act, sec. 197),

(d) **particulars of salaries of employees earning more than £10,000 per annum (sec. 8).**   Para. 19

(4) Assets comprising shares in and amounts owing by subsidiaries not consolidated and amounts owing to such subsidiaries must be shown separately in consolidated accounts.   Para. 21

In relation to such companies a statement is required giving information as set out in para. 8(7) and (8) of this chapter.

(5) Where the financial years of subsidiaries consolidated do not coincide with that of the holding company the information set out in paragraph 8 (8) of this chapter must be given.   Para. 21

EXEMPTIONS FROM PUBLIC DISCLOSURE

21. (1) **Where a company is neither a holding company nor a subsidiary, it is exempted from showing in its accounts:—**

(a) **particulars of turnover where the value does not exceed £50,000,**   Para. 13A (5) (*b*) the details of directors' emoluments mentioned in paragraph 11(2)-(5) of this chapter where the total emoluments do not exceed £7,500. Sec. 6(6)
Sec. 7(3)

(2) A company is exempted from showing in its directors' report:—

    (*a*) the value of exports where the total turnover of the company (and of its subsidiaries if any) does not exceed £50,000, Sec. 20(2)

    (*b*) the average number of employees and aggregate remuneration where the company (or the company and its subsidiaries together) employs less than 100 persons or the company is a wholly owned subsidiary of another company incorporated in Great Britain. Sec. 18(5)

(3) A company which is neither a holding company nor a subsidiary is exempted from showing in its directors' report its turnover and profit and loss before tax of each class of business, if classes differ substantially, where total turnover does not exceed £50,000. Sec. 17(1)

22. An unlimited company will not be required to annex the following documents to its annual return:—

    (*a*) certified copy of the balance sheet laid before the company in general meeting (including every document required to be annexed to the balance sheet),

    (*b*) certified copy of the auditors' report and directors' report accompanying the balance sheet,

provided that:—

    (*a*) at no time during the period to which the return relates has the unlimited company been the subsidiary of a limited company or under the control of two or more limited companies,

    (*b*) at no such time has the unlimited company been the holding company of a limited company,

    (*c*) at no such time has the unlimited company been carrying on business as the promoter of a trading stamp scheme within the meaning of the Trading Stamp Act 1964. Sec. 47

DIRECTORS' REPORT

23. Copies of the directors' report must now be sent with copies of every balance sheet and auditors' report to members of a company, holders of debentures of a company and other persons so entitled.   Sec. 24

24. The amount of information required to be disclosed in directors' reports has been extended and the full requirements are set out below:—

   (1) State of company's affairs.   1948 Act, Sec. 157(1)

   (2) Amount recommended that should be paid by way of dividend.   Sec. 157(1)

   (3) Amount proposed to be carried to reserves.   Sec. 157(1)

   (4) Principal activities of company and its subsidiaries and significant changes in those activities.   Sec. 16(1)

   (5) Names of directors at any time during year under review.   Sec. 16(1)

   (6) Significant changes in company's or its subsidiaries' fixed assets and if market value of land is substantially different from the book value an indication of the difference.   Sec. 16(1)(a)

   (7) Reason for making issue of any shares or debentures during year under review and details of classes issued and amounts received on each class.   Sec. 16(1)(b)

   (8) Contracts with the company (except service contracts) in which a director of the company has an interest, specifying parties to contract, director involved, nature of contract and nature of director's interest in contract.   Sec. 16(1)(c)

   (9) Arrangements between company and its directors whereby the directors are able to obtain benefits by the acquisition of shares or debentures of the company or any other body corporate.   Sec. 16(1)(d)

   (10) Directors'* interests (at the beginning and end of each year) in shares or debentures of the company or its group companies.   Sec. 16(1)(e)

   (11) Particulars of any matter required for an appreciation of the state of the company's affairs by its members (provided

    * Including spouses' and infant children's (sec. 31).

that, in the opinion of the directors, such disclosure would
not be harmful to the company or its subsidiaries).   Sec.
16(1)(f)

(12) Turnover and profit or loss before tax of each class of
business if classes differ substantially (see paragraph 21
of this chapter for exemption).   Sec. 17(1)

(13) Statement of:—
   (a) average number of persons employed by company
       (including subsidiaries) in each week in that year,
   (b) aggregate remuneration paid or payable in respect of
       that year to the persons by reference to whom the
       number stated under the foregoing paragraph is
       ascertained.
   This does not apply to companies with less than 100 employees or to companies which are the wholly owned
   subsidiaries of a company incorporated in Great Britain. Sec. 18

(14) Amount of contributions (if exceeding £50) given for
political and/or charitable purposes and identification of
political party which is the recipient. Such particulars
are not to be given by a wholly owned subsidiary of a
company incorporated in Great Britain: in a group such
particulars relate to contributions by the holding company
and subsidiaries between them.   Sec. 19

(15) Turnover from exports where the value exceeds £50,000
and a note where no goods are exported. Similar information is required to be given in group accounts where
the total turnover of the group exceeds £50,000.   Sec. 20

(16) Where items are shown in the directors' report instead of
in the accounts corresponding amounts for the immediately
preceding year must also be shown.   Sec. 22

INTERESTS IN SHARE CAPITAL

25. A director of a company is guilty of an offence if he (or his
spouse or infant children) purchases options to buy or sell the
right to quoted shares or debentures of the company or companies in its group.   Sec. 25
                                                       and 30

26. A director of a company must notify that company of his (or
his spouse's or infant children's) interest in any shares or
debentures in the company or its group companies and continue
to keep the company informed of any alterations in his interest

during his period of office. The company must retain a register of the information necessary to comply with these provisions. Sec. 27,
29 and 31

27. The Board of Trade may appoint an inspector to carry out an investigation of share dealings where there are circumstances suggesting that contraventions may have occurred in relation to the requirements referred to in paragraphs 25 and 26 of this chapter. Sec. 32

28. Every person, who becomes interested in shares carrying unrestricted rights to vote at the Annual General Meeting in a quoted company of an amount equal to one-tenth or more of the nominal value of the voting share capital of the company, must notify the company in writing of the existence of the interest together with the occurrence of events which give rise to changes. Subsequent acquisitions and disposals must also be notified to the company, which must keep a register of the identities of shareholders who fall into the above category. Sec. 33
and 34

DIRECTORS' SERVICE CONTRACTS

29. Each company must keep a copy of any written contract of service with a director, or a memorandum setting out the terms of a contract, where the contract is not in writing. These contracts and memoranda are to be open to the inspection of any member of the company, without charge but need not be kept if the director is required to work wholly or mainly outside the U.K. or the contract is to be in force for less than 12 months. Sec. 26

QUALIFICATION OF AUDITORS

30. (1) For companies the auditor must be either a member of a body of accountants established in the United Kingdom and for the time being recognised by the Board of Trade *or* authorised by the Board of Trade to be appointed either as having similar qualifications obtained outside the United Kingdom or as having obtained adequate knowledge and experience in the course of his employment by a member of a recognised body of accountants or as having before August 6, 1947, practised in Great

Britain as an accountant. An auditor cannot be an officer or servant of the company, a person who is a partner of or in the employment of an officer or servant of the company, or a body corporate.

(2) A person shall also not be qualified for appointment as auditor of a company if he is disqualified for appointment as auditor of that company's subsidiary company or holding company.

(3) A Scottish firm is qualified for appointment as auditor of a company if all the partners are qualified for appointment as auditor of the company.

1948 Act, Sec. 161

31. If no shares or debentures of a company or of a body corporate of which it is a subsidiary have been quoted on a stock exchange or offered to the public, a person shall be qualified for appointment as auditor of that company if he is authorised by the Board of Trade by reason of his being in practice as an accountant for the year ended November 3, 1966, and being the auditor of an exempt private company on that day.

Sec. 13(1)

32. Any auditor of an exempt private company remains qualified for appointment as auditor until twelve months have elapsed from January 27, 1968 (the date on which the repeal took effect) provided the condition mentioned in paragraph 31 with respect to shares and debentures is satisfied at the time of his appointment.

Sec. 13(2)

33. The provision whereby a partner of, or a person in the employment of, an officer or servant of a company can be auditor of an exempt private company will continue to exist in the case of duly appointed existing auditors until three years have elapsed from the date on which the repeal took effect provided the condition mentioned in paragraph 31 with respect to shares and debentures is satisfied at the time of his appointment.

Sec. 13(3)

34. A person shall not be authorised under section 161 of the 1968 Act by Board of Trade to be appointed as auditor of a company as having before August 6, 1947, practised in Great Britain as an accountant unless he has made an application in that behalf to the Board of Trade before January 27, 1968 (the date on which this subsection comes into operation).

Sec. 13(4)

AUDITORS' REPORT

35. The form of the auditors' report has been amended as a result of the Companies Act 1967 and the auditor must now report (**except in the case of a company that is entitled to avail itself of Part III of the eighth schedule of the 1948 Act**) whether in his opinion the company's balance sheet and profit and loss account and (if it is a holding company submitting group accounts) the group accounts have been properly prepared in accordance with the provisions of the Companies Act 1948 **and the Companies Act 1967** and whether in his opinion a true and fair view is given:—

   (a) in the case of the balance sheet, of the state of the company's affairs as at the end of its financial year,

   (b) in the case of the profit and loss account (if it be not framed as a consolidated profit and loss account) of the company's profit and loss for its financial year,

   (c) in the case of group accounts submitted by a holding company, of the state of affairs and profit or loss of the company and its subsidiaries dealt with thereby, so far as concerns members of the company.   Sec. 14(3)

36. **It is the duty of the auditors of a company, in preparing their report, to carry out such investigations as will enable them to form an opinion as to:—**

   (1) **whether proper books of account have been kept by the company and proper returns adequate for their audit have been received from branches not visited by them, and**

   (2) **whether the company's balance sheet and (unless it is framed as a consolidated profit and loss account) profit and loss account are in agreement with the books of account and returns, and if the auditors are of opinion that proper books of account have not been kept by the company or that proper returns adequate for their audit have not been received from branches not visited by them, or if the balance sheet and (unless it is framed as a consolidated profit and loss account) profit and loss account are not in agreement with the books of account, the auditors shall state that fact in their report.**   Sec. 14(4)

37. If the auditors fail to obtain all the information and explanations which, to the best of their knowledge and belief, are necessary for the purposes of their audit, they shall state that fact in their report.   Sec. 14(6)

38. It is the auditors' duty to include in their report a statement giving the particulars required to be disclosed in respect of the following cases, where the information has not been given in the accounts:—

   (a) directors' emoluments (48 Act, sec. 196 and sec. 6),
   (b) directors' emoluments, the rights to receive which have been waived (sec. 7),
   (c) salaries of employees receiving more than £10,000 a year (sec. 8), and
   (d) loans to officers (48 Act, sec. 197).

39. Auditors are entitled:—

   (a) to attend general meetings,
   (b) to receive notices and other communications relating to general meetings, and
   (c) to be heard at any general meeting.   Sec. 14(7)

ABOLITION OF STATUS OF EXEMPT PRIVATE COMPANY

40. The status of exempt private company has been abolished and those companies which previously enjoyed that status are now subject to all the provisions of the Act unless exempted on the lines indicated in paragraph 21 of this chapter.   Sec. 2

RE-REGISTRATION OF LIMITED COMPANY AS UNLIMITED

41. A company registered as limited may be re-registered as unlimited. Details of the procedure are given in paragraphs 16 and 17 of Chapter III.

42. An unlimited company is excepted from the requirement to annex accounts to the annual return if, during the period under review:—

    (a) the company has not been the subsidiary of a limited company,

    (b) the company has not been the holding company of a limited company, and

    (c) the company has not been carrying on the business as the promoter of a trading stamp scheme within the meaning of the Trading Stamp Act 1964.   Sec. 47

RE-REGISTRATION OF UNLIMITED COMPANY AS LIMITED

43. A company registered as unlimited may be re-registered as limited. Details of the procedure are given in paragraphs 18 to 20 of Chapter III.   Sec. 44

PARTNERSHIPS OF MORE THAN 20 PERSONS

44. Members within each of the following groups may form partner-ships of more than 20 persons:—

    (a) practising solicitors, provided each partner is a solicitor;

    (b) practising accountants, provided each partner falls within the terms of either paragraph (a) or paragraph (b) of section 161(1) of the Companies Act 1948;

    (c) members of a recognised stock exchange, provided each partner is a member of that exchange; and

    (d) any other groups who for this purpose are approved under regulations made by the Board of Trade.   Sec. 120

INSPECTION

45. The Board of Trade's powers of enquiry not only cover com-panies incorporated in Great Britain but extend to companies incorporated abroad carrying on business in Great Britain.   Sec. 42

46. The Board of Trade may require any company to produce such books or papers as may be specified and may require such books or papers to be produced forthwith by either a representative of the company or any person who appears to be in possession of the required documents. Production by a person who has a lien on the books or papers is without prejudice to the lien. The Board of Trade's powers include taking copies of books or papers and seeking explanations with regard to them. Where books or papers are not produced, the person required to produce them may be asked to state, to the best of his knowledge and belief, where they are.   Sec. 109

47. (1) The Board of Trade may obtain a warrant to enter and search premises where there are reasonable grounds for suspecting that books and papers, asked for but not produced, can be found.   Sec. 110(1)

    (2) The Board of Trade may retain books and papers found for a period of three months or until the conclusion of any proceedings arising from the investigation.   Sec. 110(3)

    (3) The Board of Trade may not publish or disclose any of the information obtained without receiving written consent from the company unless the publication or disclosure is required in certain specified circumstances.   Sec. 111

48. The Board of Trade may present a petition to wind up a company where it is just and equitable to do so on the grounds that it would be in the public interest. A petition to wind up may also be made where it appears to the Board that there is oppression of a particular section of the members.   Sec. 35

49. It is no longer necessary for the Board of Trade to refer to the Director of Public Prosecutions or the Lord Advocate to decide whether to prosecute if there is evidence of a criminal offence.   Sec. 36

50. The Board of Trade may bring civil proceedings in the name of and on behalf of a company where it appears to the Board to be necessary in the public interest.   Sec. 37

51. (1) The Board of Trade may appoint inspectors to investigate the affairs of a company where there are circumstances suggesting that the business is being or has been conducted with intent to defraud. This has effect even if the company is in the course of being voluntarily wound up.   Sec. 38

   (2) The inspectors have power to insist upon the attendance of officers or agents of companies under investigation.   Sec. 39

   (3) An inspector may without making an interim report inform the Board of Trade of any matters arising during his investigation which tend to show that an offence has been committed.   Sec. 41

52. Answers to some questions arising in relation to inspections may be used in evidence against the individual giving them.   Sec. 50

53. Exemption is given to solicitors and bankers from producing certain information.   Sec. 116

54. Sections 164 to 168 and 170 (as amended) to 175 of the Companies Act 1948 still apply to companies incorporated in the United Kingdom.

TIME-TABLE OF DATES FROM WHICH THE PROVISIONS OF THE COMPANIES ACT 1967 TAKE EFFECT   Sec. 57

55. Commencing three months from date of enactment:—

   (a) Penalisation of directors dealing in certain options and provision for securing certain material facts concerning directors' interests.   Secs. 25 to 32

   (b) Provisions for securing disclosure of substantial individual interests in share capital carrying unrestricted voting rights in quoted companies.   Secs. 33 and 34 (*c*) Re-registration of limited companies as unlimited and registration or re-registration of unlimited companies as limited.

Secs. 43 to 45

(*d*) New scale of registration fees (see pages 32 and 33).

Sec. 48 and Sch. 3

56. Commencing six months from date of enactment:—

(*a*) Abolition of status of exempt private company.

Sec. 2

(*b*) Disclosure in accounts.

Secs. 3 to 12 and Schs. 1 and 2

(*c*) Qualification for appointment as auditor and auditors' report.

Secs. 13 and 14

(*d*) Matters in connection with the directors' report (except analysis into classes of turnover and profitability).

Secs. 15, 16 and 18 to 24

57. Commencing twelve months from date of enactment:—

Analysis of turnover and profitability of each class of business. Sec. 17

SCALE OF REGISTRATION FEES

(This is schedule 3 reproduced from the Companies Act 1967 by kind permission of H.M. Stationery Office and references to "this Act" refer to the Companies Act 1967.)

PART I

TABLE OF FEES

Matter in respect of which Fee is payable	Amount of Fee
For registration on its formation under the principal Act of a company as one limited by shares, registration under that Act in pursuance of Part VIII thereof of a company as one so limited (not being a company in whose case the liability of the members thereof was, before registration in pursuance of that Part, limited by some other Act or by letters patent) or re-registration under the principal Act in pursuance of section 33 of this Act of a company as one limited by shares.	If the nominal capital does not exceed £2,000, the sum of £20. If the nominal capital exceeds £2,000 but does not exceed £5,000, the sum of £20 with the addition of £1 for each £1,000 or part of £1,000 of nominal capital in excess of £2,000. If the nominal capital exceeds £5,000 but does not exceed £100,000, the sum of £23 with the addition of 5s. for each £1,000 or part of nominal capital in excess of £5,000. If the nominal capital exceeds £100,000, the sum of £46, 15s., with the addition of 1s. for each £1,000 or part of £1,000 of nominal capital in excess of £100,000.
For registration on its formation under the principal Act of a company as one not having a share capital, registration under that Act in pursuance of Part VIII thereof of a company as one limited by guarantee and not having a share capital or re-registration under that Act in pursuance of section 33 of this Act of a company as one so limited and not having a share capital.	If the number of members stated in the articles does not exceed 25, the sum of £20. If the number of members stated in the articles exceeds 25, but does not exceed 100, the sum of £20, with the addition of £1 for each 25 members or fraction of 25 members in excess of the first 25. If the number of members stated in the articles exceeds 100 but is not stated to be unlimited, the sum of £23 with the addition of 5s. for each 50 members or fraction of 50 members after the first 100. If the number of members is stated in the articles to be unlimited, the sum of £38.
For registration on its formation under the principal Act of a company as one limited by guarantee and having a share capital, or registration under that Act in pursuance of Part VIII thereof of a company as one so limited and having a share capital, registration under that Act in pursuance of Part VIII thereof of a company as one so limited and having a share capital or re-registration under that Act in pursuance of section 33 of this Act of a company as one limited by guarantee and having a share capital.	The same amount as would be charged for registration if the company were limited by shares or the same amount as would be so charged if the company had not a share capital, whichever is the higher.
For re-registration of a company under the principal Act in pursuance of section 32 of this Act.	£5.

C   For registration of an increase in the share capital of a company.

An amount equal to the difference (if any) between the amount which, were the company being registered on its formation under the principal Act, would be payable by reference to its capital as increased and the amount which, were the company being so registered would be payable by reference to its capital immediately before the increase.

For registration of an increase in the membership of a company limited by guarantee or an unlimited company.

An amount equal to the difference (if any) between the amount which, were the company being registered on its formation under the principal Act as a company limited by guarantee or as an unlimited company, would be payable by reference to its membership as increased and the amount which, were the company being so registered as such a company, would be payable by reference to its membership immediately before the increase.

For registration of a copy of an annual return or copies of documents delivered to the registrar of companies in compliance with section 410 of the principal Act.

£3.

For entering on the register the name of a company assumed by virtue of the passing of a special resolution by virtue of section 18(1) of the principal Act.

£10.

PART II

LIMITATIONS ON OPERATION OF PART I

1. Where, in the case of a company limited by guarantee and having a share capital or an unlimited company having a share capital, an increase of share capital is made at the same time as an increase of membership, the company shall pay whichever fee is the higher, but not both.

2. The total of the fees to be paid by a company by reference to its membership shall in no case exceed £38.

3. The total of the fees to be paid by a company by reference to its share capital or of the fees to be paid by it by reference to its membership and the fees to be paid by it by reference to its share capital shall in no case exceed £68.

4. In determining what fee (if any) is to be paid by a company upon an increase in its membership it shall be assumed, for the purpose of the application of the foregoing provisions of this part of this Schedule, that the amount that would be payable by it by reference to its membership immediately before the increase has been paid, and in determining what fee (if any) is to be paid by a company upon an increase in its share capital it shall be assumed for that purpose that the amount that would be payable by it by reference to its capital immediately before the increase has been paid.

CHAPTER II

REQUIREMENTS ON DISCLOSURE

INTRODUCTION

1. This chapter considers some of the problems that are likely to be met in practice as a result of the disclosure requirements of the new Act. It is not intended to be comprehensive. Not every requirement is mentioned, nor every possibility explored; other solutions than those suggested here will often be acceptable. The main intention of this article is to point out doubts and difficulties.

2. The disclosure requirements for unlimited companies are no different from those of limited companies. The only difference is that unlimited companies do not have to attach copies of their accounts, auditors' or directors' reports to the annual return lodged with the Registrar; this exemption lasts as long as they have neither controlled nor been under the control of a limited company or companies during the period to which the return relates (sec. 47(1)). The distinction therefore turns, not on what is disclosed, but on whom it is disclosed to.

3. This chapter does not cover the provisions relating to special classes of company—banks, insurance and shipping companies.

DISCLOSURE IN ACCOUNTS
BALANCE SHEET
FIXED ASSETS

4. For most kinds of fixed assets included in the accounts at a valuation, there will have to be disclosed the years of the valuations and " the several values ", *i.e.* the values applicable to each year; these requirements are subject to the saving " so far as they are known to the directors " (sch. 2, para. 11(6A)). Where individual properties have been valued at different times it should be practicable to give the written-down value of each. Where, however, the plant and machinery has been revalued at one or more times in the past the required information will not usually be available, as plant registers generally segregate items by

location or department rather than by date; it should be sufficient in such cases to state that it is not practicable to obtain the necessary information.

5. In the year in which fixed assets are revalued the accounts must give particulars of the valuers or their qualifications and of " the bases of valuation used by them " (sch. 2, para. 11(6A)). The disclosure should make clear whether the valuation has been made on the basis of existing use, and what allowance has been or is to be made for capital gains tax and betterment levy.

6. The total movements during the year on fixed assets other than investments have to be disclosed (sch. 2, para. 11(6B)). It is helpful if capital expenditure is distinguished from additions arising through acquisitions of new subsidiaries and revaluation increments. Similar movements on depreciation are not required by the Act but should preferably be given.

7. The figure of " land " appearing in the balance sheet as a fixed asset has to be divided between freeholds, long leases and short leases (sch. 2, para. 11(6c)). Where land and buildings are shown as one figure it would be reasonable to split only the total in this way. Crownholds are not referred to, but should be shown separately if material. The distinction between long and short leases rests on whether fifty years or more remain unexpired at the balance sheet date, not, as formerly for tax purposes, on whether there were fifty years or more to run from the original grant of the lease (sch. 2, para. 29). A lease includes an agreement for a lease; thus a short term building agreement to grant a long lease on satisfactory completion is for this purpose a long and not a short lease. The only obligatory information to be given about leases is the portion of the asset account attributable to them, so that if no premiums have been paid, no disclosure need be made; it may, however, assist understanding to show material amounts of rents paid.

8. Capital expenditure "authorised by the directors" has to be disclosed, if material, as well as that contracted for (sch. 2, para. 11(6)). The concept of "authorisation" should preferably be limited to expenditure that will be contracted for within a reasonable time, or that forms part of a scheme that will reasonably soon be started. Otherwise it might reflect little more than pipe-dreams.

9. Assets are to be identified as fixed, current or—a new category —neither (sch. 2, para. 4(2)). It should be sufficient to indicate the last class by exception, being those assets not labelled either "fixed" or "current". Examples could be debts not due within a year, or inter-company accounts with an indefinite repayment date.

SUBSIDIARIES

10. A list is required of material subsidiaries' names and countries of incorporation (if other than Great Britain) and of the proportion of each class of shares held by the parent company in them; this forms part of the accounts (sec. 3(1)). If the parent company is registered in Scotland and any material subsidiary in England, or *vice versa*, this must be stated (sec. 3(1)(*b*)). If the number of subsidiaries is prohibitively large the list may be confined to the principal ones only (sec. 3(4)). A statement is also required of the principal activities of the subsidiaries, and of any changes in them during the year; this forms part of the directors' report (sec. 16(1)). If the two requirements are combined in the one schedule the auditors' report may have to be carefully worded to specify exactly what is covered by it.

11. The list of interests in subsidiaries must distinguish the shares held by the parent company from those held by intermediate subsidiaries (sec. 3(2)). Although not strictly required by the Act, it will be helpful to show only the group's ultimate interest in sub-subsidiaries owned by partly-owned intermediate subsidiaries.

12. Subsidiaries trading or incorporated overseas may be omitted from the list if the directors think that to include them would be harmful and the Board of Trade agrees (sec. 3(3)). Where advantage of this exemption is taken some indication that there has been an omission should preferably be given: such an acknowledgement is obligatory where subsidiaries are left out on the grounds of immateriality (sec. 3(4) and (5)).

INVESTMENTS

13. The 1948 Act laid down three categories of investment—trade investments, other investments that were quoted and others that were not. The 1967 Act abolishes the category of trade investments. It applies only two criteria, but applies both of them to *each* investment:

    (i) is it quoted or unquoted?
    (ii) is more than 10% of the equity owned?

The answer to (i) does not determine the answer to (ii); according as they are quoted or unquoted certain consequences follow regardless of whether more than 10% is owned or less.

14. The balance sheet must show separately the amounts of quoted and unquoted investments (sch. 2, para 8(1)(a)). As before, this does not include holdings in subsidiaries (sch. 2, para. 15(2)(a)), but by contrast quoted investments can now include trade investments. Quoted and unquoted should therefore be shown separately under each heading required—associated companies, marketable investments, other investments—bearing in mind the overriding requirement to distinguish fixed, current and other assets.

15. There is only one further requirement for quoted investments (whether 10% owned or not). That is to show their " *aggregate* market value " where different from the carrying value; it would, however, plainly be right to give the separate market value of each category shown separately (sch. 2, para. 11(8)). It follows that even the market value of long-term investments which there is no intention of getting rid of should be disclosed.

16. There are two further requirements for unquoted investments (whether 10% owned or not). First, cost and aggregate amounts written off must, as at present, be shown (sch. 2, paras. 5(1) and 5(2)(c)). Secondly, for equity shares only, there must be shown in total the income receivable during the year, the company's share of the underlying profits less losses (before and after tax) in their latest financial years for which accounts have been received, its share of their undistributed profits less losses since they were acquired, and the manner in which losses have been dealt with

in the company's own accounts (sch. 2, para. 5A). Both these requirements are avoided if the directors give in lieu their estimate of the individual or collective values of the investments; they may well decide to do so for the sake of simplicity.

17. The information discussed so far has to be given in any event. For investments in which more than 10% of any class of equity capital is held further information has to be given as well (sec. 4(1)). This comprises the companies' names, their countries of incorporation (if other than Great Britain), their registration in England if the owning company is registered in Scotland and *vice versa*, and the nature and extent of the *total* holdings in them, similar to the requirements on subsidiaries (para. 10 above). It is to be noted that a 10% holding in any *one* class of equity share requires disclosure of *all* other holdings in that company. " Equity share " is defined as in the 1948 Act, sec. 154(5), and therefore includes certain participating preference shares.

18. There is no provision in the 10% equity capital rule for taking account of loan capital or for disclosing separately the amount of any loans however large. It is suggested, however, that loans should preferably be shown separately where—as often—they provide the associate with a significant source of capital.

19. Even though 10% of any class of equity share is not held, that is not the end of the matter: a further calculation must also be made, to see if the amount at which any one investment in shares is stated in the balance sheet exceeds 10% of the assets—that is, of the assets of the company owning the shares. If it does, similar information on name, country of incorporation, etc., and proportion of shares held must be given (sec. 4(2)). This is again a provision dealing with shares only, not with the *total* investment in shares plus loans. It is not stated whether the comparison is with the gross or net assets of the owning company, although it *is* stated that those assets are to be taken at their balance sheet values. The intention of the section is no doubt to disclose individual holdings which are material in relation to the company holding them, and this would encourage the interpretation of net rather than gross assets; but in view of the wording of the section, objection could scarcely be taken to the contrary opinion.

20. For both 10% calculations—that is, 10% of each class of equity share and 10% of the owning company's assets—shareholdings in the one investment held throughout a group are *not* aggregated (sec. 4(7)). There must be separate calculations for the parent and for each subsidiary's holdings in the one investment, and only those which individually exceed the 10% rule will be disclosed separately in each company's own accounts. The separate disclosures do *not* have to be combined in the consolidated accounts (sch. 2, para. 19), although it seems preferable that they should be; otherwise substantial holdings held by subsidiary companies will not be disclosed to the parent company's members.

21. Similar exemptions for overseas and too-numerous holdings in 10% associates apply as for subsidiaries, and similar notice of any omissions made should be given in the accounts (sec. 4(3) and (4) and para. 12 above).

22. The provisions on 10% associates apply only to holdings in bodies corporate (sec. 4(1)). Interests in a partnership would therefore not require to be disclosed, but should be if material.

STOCK AND WORK IN PROGRESS
23. The manner of computing stock and work in progress, if the figure is material, is to be explained (sch. 2, para. 11(8B)). It is suggested that one of two kinds of explanation should be attempted: either it should be kept as short as possible, thus demonstrating that details have not been given because they are not necessary or not helpful, or it should give full and *specific* information on what the method of calculation is and what it has been applied to. Generalities are permissible provided they are short. There will usually be a distinction between retailing or merchanting companies on the one hand and manufacturing or processing companies on the other. Examples of acceptable wording for retailers or merchants could be " at cost ", or " at lower of cost and net realisable value ". An example for a manufacturer could be " finished goods and work in progress at 196– standard cost including fixed manufacturing overheads on the basis of budgeted normal production, excluding selling, administration, finance and research overheads, and reduced to net realisable

value where lower; and raw materials at average purchase price including carriage and duty, reduced to net replacement cost where lower ". It is desirable to avoid an appearance of explanation that seems to convey more than it does, *e.g.* " Stock has been valued at the lower of cost or market value on a number of bases suitable to the business which are substantially consistent with those of earlier years and which include, where appropriate, a proportion of applicable overheads ". If the bases had not been suitable, consistent or appropriate, the auditors would have had to say so.

24. For large groups and those comprising a number of different types of business, the minimum of explanation is likely to be the most that is meaningful.

LOANS

25. Bank loans and overdrafts have to be shown separately as at present; in addition, the aggregate amount of loans made to the company repayable in whole or in part more than five years from the balance sheet date must be given, with summarised particulars of the redemption terms and interest rates (sch. 2, paras. 8(1)(*d*) and (4)). Shorter non-bank loans thus do not have to be shown, but it is good practice to show material ones; this distinguishes them from liabilities arising in the ordinary course of business, and mitigates the importance of deciding whether marginal institutions are " banks " or not. A loan is held for this purpose to fall due for repayment on the earliest date the lender could call for it—on the assumption, if necessary, that he exercised all options open to him (sch. 2, para. 30).

26. There seems to be no reason to restrict the word "loan" only to those balances arising where cash has passed. It will be helpful to include every repayable balance which arose otherwise than in the ordinary course of business and by which the company's assets are in whole or in part financed.

DIVIDENDS

27. Proposed dividends have to be shown gross, before deduction of income tax, in the balance sheet and profit and loss account (sch. 2, paras. 8(1)(*e*) and 12(1)(*h*)). Where relief is due for

income tax deducted from franked investment income, the full gross amount of the dividend proposed will not in fact be payable. Further, some companies are likely to wish to show their dividends in two parts in the profit and loss account, so as to distinguish the net amount going to the shareholders from the income tax going to the Inland Revenue; the tax under this treatment may be grouped with, or set off against, other tax items in the balance sheet. In such cases the gross amount of the dividends can be shown inset, or as an addition of the tax and net figures.

RESERVES

28. The requirement to distinguish between capital and revenue reserves has been abolished by the new Act (sch. 2, paras. 6 and 27(1)). This is a change only in what must be disclosed; it does not affect what is legally distributable, nor what the directors may consider not to be distributable. It may therefore still be helpful to distinguish two kinds of reserve. In general, a distinction based on *provenance* or source rather than distributability or possible destination is likely to be more meaningful: it is sensible to ask how much of the net assets came from ordinary retentions, how much from capital profits and how much from revaluation surpluses.

29. The obligation to show the share premium account separately is unaffected (sch. 2, para. 2(c)). Special reserve accounts which have to be maintained under the articles or loan agreements should also still be disclosed separately—*e.g.* a debenture redemption reserve. It is only where the distinction between capital and revenue reserves has become meaningless that advantage should be taken to combine them—*e.g.* where the origins of both have been lost in history and as they are alike invested permanently in the business neither is available for distribution.

ULTIMATE PARENT

30. Where a company is a subsidiary, the accounts must state the name and country of incorporation of the company regarded by the directors as the ultimate parent (sec. 5(1)). This will present problems when the directors do not know the facts. Have they a duty to make enquiries? To pursue them if rebuffed?

To guess ? Similar problems can be met under the present Stock Exchange requirement for quoted companies to state whether they are close or not. It is suggested that directors will normally discharge their duty under this section if they ask the controlling shareholders and pass on the reply.

31. There is an exemption for subsidiaries carrying on business overseas if disclosure would be harmful and the Board of Trade consent (sec. 5(2)). There is, however, no exemption for U.K. subsidiaries on the grounds that the ultimate parent is an overseas company.

PROFIT AND LOSS ACCOUNT
TURNOVER

32. All turnover is to be disclosed, except that attributable to the business of banking, discounting or such other class as may be prescribed (sch. 2, para. 13A). Presumably other classes would be prescribed in statutory instruments by the Board of Trade as they already have the power to alter the 8th schedule in this way (1948 Act, sec. 454(1)). The fact that there have been omissions must be disclosed.

33. " Turnover " is not defined, but the method by which it is arrived at is to be stated (sch. 2, para. 13A). Provided its meaning in each set of accounts is made quite clear there is room for variety in this. Goods invoiced on dispatch are straightforward. For agency businesses it will no doubt mean fees and charges billed. For companies hiring or leasing plant it would be helpful to distinguish income accruing during the period from new contracts entered into. For businesses paying and recouping large sums in excise and similar duties these should be shown separately. For long-term contracting businesses the certified or selling value of work done is likely to be a better guide to output than what has actually been invoiced; where profits are brought in only on completion it will be relevant to show also the value of work completed during the year. It seems right to look in each business for the best measure of activity there is, and to use that, suitably described, as the " turnover ".

34. It is suggested that inter-group sales should be shown separately, both to assist the true and fair view and to make it easy to eliminate them on consolidation.

35. There is an exemption for certain small companies. It is important to appreciate that in the new Act there is no *general* criterion for deciding whether a company is small, and if it is, for exempting it from a specified number of the obligations to disclose. Where smallness is considered to be relevant in relation to any one disclosure requirement, it is defined only in relation to that requirement; where it is deemed to be relevant to another, it is defined in relation to that other. In no case does exemption from one requirement automatically entail exemption from any others, apart from consequential matters. Each possibility of exemption must therefore be looked at independently. In the case of turnover, a company which is neither a holding nor a subsidiary company is exempted from disclosing its turnover if the figure does not exceed £50,000 (sch. 2, para. 13A(5)). Comparison may be made with paragraph 37 below for an analogous exemption on directors' emoluments where the amount of the emoluments is small.

DIRECTORS' EMOLUMENTS

36. The new requirements to show the emoluments of the chairman, the most highly paid director receiving more than him, and the number of directors in each £2,500 band are *in addition to* the existing requirements to show total remuneration, pensions, and so on (sec. 6(1) and (2) and 1948 Act, sec. 196). It is awkward that the new requirements call for an analysis of emoluments which in two respects can (and generally will) be *less* than the emoluments that must continue to be disclosed in aggregate under the existing law:—

(a) Contributions paid on behalf of directors under any pension scheme are left out of the analysis—no doubt because it could be difficult in practice to allocate them fairly to individuals (sec. 6(3)).

(b) The emoluments of the chairman or of any director are similarly left out of the analysis if he discharged his duties wholly or mainly outside the United Kingdom (sec. 6(1)(a) and (b) and (2)).

It will therefore be wise to see whether the number of directors shown in each bracket could in fact account for the total emoluments shown. If not, the short-fall must be attributable to one or both of the above reasons and the wording introducing the analysis should make this clear.

37. Nil returns in any intermediate £2,500 bracket are not required. In group accounts, the analysis by brackets is required for the chairman and directors of the parent company only, but taking account of their remuneration from every source (sch. 2, para. 19). There is no exemption for subsidiaries, wholly-owned or otherwise, but there is an exemption for certain " small " companies (cf. paragraph 35 above). A company which is neither a holding nor a subsidiary company is exempted from disclosing the analysis of directors' emoluments by £2,500 bands as long as the total of the emoluments shown in the accounts does not exceed £7,500 (sec. 6(6)). The total amount of directors' emoluments must continue to be disclosed in the accounts of every limited company as at present; in future, however, this information will without exception be open to the public gaze at the office of the Registrar, and where the total exceeds £7,500 the emoluments of the chairman (and of the most highly-paid director receiving more than him if any) and the analysis by £2,500 bands will be available as well.

TOP EXECUTIVES' EMOLUMENTS

38. The number of executives other than directors in each £2,500 band over £10,000 must be shown (sec. 8(1)). As with the analysis of directors' emoluments, those working wholly or mainly outside the U.K. are excluded and pension contributions are left out of emoluments (sec. 8(1)(b) and (2)). There appears to be no need to give a nil return. This section applies only to " persons in the *company's* employment ", but all their emoluments must be shown, from whatever source or company they have been paid (sec. 8(2)). There is no requirement to incorporate the subsidiaries' figures in the consolidated accounts (sch. 2, para. 19). It follows that disclosure will be made in the group accounts only for those executives who are in the employment of the *parent* company. A company divided into operating divisions will therefore have to make disclosure to its members for all its top executives; a parent company which acts as a holding company only, with the top managers employed *wholly* by subsidiaries, will not need to make such disclosure for any. Each of the subsidiaries will of course have

to make this disclosure in its own accounts for the executives employed by it.

INTEREST AND HIRE CHARGES

39. It is no longer necessary to show separately interest paid on debentures and fixed loans (sch. 2, para. 12(1)(b)). Three headings of interest charged are to be given:—

    (a) Interest on bank loans and overdrafts. It is considered that these can be shown as one total, though the wording of the section might suggest that they had to be shown as two.

    (b) Interest on loans payable wholly within five years from the balance sheet date. This gives a further reason for disclosing such loans in the balance sheet (suggested in para. 25 above).

    (c) Interest on all other loans, i.e. those repayable wholly or partly more than five years from the balance sheet date.

No distinction is made in the Act between interest on secured loans and interest on other loans.

40. The amount charged for the " hire of plant and machinery " must, if material, be shown separately (sch. 2, para.12(1)(gb)). This is so, however short the hire or long the lease. It is suggested that the words " plant and machinery " should be widely construed, to cover all kinds of equipment used for the purposes of the business—e.g. buses, furniture, vehicles, ships. Inconsistencies will occur, and if significant should be explained; the amount payable for hire under a hire-purchase contract will presumably be restricted to the interest loading only, since the write-off of the capital cost will be included as depreciation, whereas the amount payable for hire under a leasing contract will be everything due under it. It seems anomalous that the amount charged for leasing property other than plant and machinery is not required to be shown by the Act.

41. There is no requirement in the Act to show interest receivable, except in so far as it constitutes income from quoted or unquoted investments (sch. 2, para. 12(1)(g)). It is doubtful whether every loan can be said to constitute an " investment ", but permanent

ones should be so treated. It is suggested that significant amounts of interest receivable should be shown separately, distinguishing interest on loans to associated companies from other kinds of interest.

RENTS RECEIVABLE

42. Rents payable do not have to be disclosed, whereas if rents receivable on land, net of outgoings, form a substantial part of the company's revenue they do (sch. 2, para. 12(1)(*ga*)). This is the converse of interest, where the general rule is that what is payable must be shown but not what is receivable. It can, however, be a meaningful addition to the true and fair view to show the amount of rent payable when it is large.

TAX

43. It is no longer obligatory to include overseas tax as United Kingdom tax to the extent that double tax relief is obtained for it; the amount of overseas tax which is effectively relieved can be shown, if desired, as a separate item (sch. 2, para. 12(1)(*c*)). The total charge for overseas tax has to be disclosed as well as the U.K. charge, and also the amount the U.K. charge would have been but for double tax relief. The following lay-out appears to satisfy these requirements sufficiently:—

U.K. corporation tax (*i.e.* on income arising in U.K. or on overseas income not covered by double tax relief)				x x x	
Overseas tax:					
For which double tax relief against U.K. corporation tax is obtained	x x x				
Not so relieved	x x x				
		——————	x x x		
Total tax charge				x x x	

There seems to be no objection, however, to continuing the existing practice of including overseas tax for which relief is obtained as part of the U.K. charge and showing the double tax relief as a credit.

44. The charge for United Kingdom income tax has to be disclosed (sch. 2, para. 12(1)(c)). The usual elements of income tax payable by companies will be two: first, tax suffered on franked investment income received; secondly, schedule F on distributions less relief for the tax on the franked investment income. This is a subject on which differing views can be held, but it is submitted that where franked investment income is material each of these should be separately disclosed in the profit and loss account, since one is a tax on income and the other a tax on distributions. Where franked investment income is small, however, it should not be necessary to include both the off-setting income tax charge and relief in the profit and loss account; its amount can be revealed, if desired, by way of note. The Act requires dividends to be shown at their gross amount before deduction of income tax, possibly leaving the schedule F content to be inferred (sch. 2, para. 12(1)(h)); as mentioned in paragraph 27 above, however, a number of companies will no doubt wish to show dividends payable in their two constituent parts of tax and net amount. Further profit and loss charges for U.K. income tax will be met in close companies where there are assessments on short-falls or loans to participators that have been written off.

45. An interesting requirement of the new Act is that the accounts must state any " special circumstances " which have affected liability to tax (whether on profits or capital gains) in the latest financial year or which will so affect it in the future (sch. 2, para. 14(3A)). Significant matters of this kind could include losses forward; group relief for losses (in the individual companies' accounts only); tax on capital gains deferred by the " roll-over " provisions; inter-company dividends caught as dividend-stripping; tax on the remittance of overseas profits earned in earlier years; depreciation on a revaluation increment not allowable for tax, or material discrepancies between depreciation and writing down allowances not covered by an equalisation account; large disallowable items; contingent capital gains liability on a revaluation surplus; interest to participators and excess directors' remuneration in close companies not allowed for tax; and amounts set aside as provisions not allowed for tax until paid. It is suggested that such disclosures should be restricted to cases where the tax effect is large enough to be really important.

46. There appears to be no obligation to show corporation tax on capital profits taken direct to reserve other than the general obligation to show reserve movements, but it is considered that it is good practice to show this where material.

PRIOR YEARS

47. Charges and credits arising from events occurring in previous years are to be shown separately if not included with other matters (sch. 2, para. 12A). This is in addition to—and presumably in amplification of—the existing requirement that profit and loss transactions of an exceptional or non-recurrent nature should be separately disclosed (sch. 2, para. 14(6)(a)). The intention of the Act is perhaps that all prior years' items should be passed through the profit and loss account at some stage and not taken straight to reserve, but it is doubtful whether its wording is apt to make this obligatory. The Act does not allow set-off between the ups and the downs and would therefore not permit setting tax relief against the item it relates to unless the amount was disclosed. It is suggested that this provision should be reserved for individual items of real significance and substance, rather than accumulating a large number of small pluses and minuses.

GENERAL

48. The new Act makes regrettably little provision for excluding disclosure on grounds of immateriality. Nevertheless, the over-riding requirement must be to give a true and fair view, and this should encourage such exclusions wherever it is sensible to make them. There is a common-sense distinction between items which are of interest to the shareholders even though they are relatively immaterial in relation to the significant figures in the accounts (*e.g.* directors' remuneration), and items which are only of interest to the shareholders if they are themselves of a significant size (*e.g.* quoted investments). It is difficult for a reader to see what is important in a complex set of accounts if he is continually being bemused with trifles.

49. Apart from exemptions for special classes of company like banks, for certain disclosures regarding overseas holdings and for provisions where the Board of Trade give consent, there are

only two general exemptions affecting the accounts and these are
both for small companies (although they are " small " in different
ways): non-group companies whose turnover does not exceed
£50,000 do not need to disclose it (paragraph 35 above); and
non-group companies whose directors' emoluments do not exceed
£7,500, while still having to disclose them in total, do not need
to give the analysis into £2,500 bands (paragraph 37 above). Otherwise all the statutory requirements must be observed in every set of
accounts for every company, however small it may be and whether
or not it is a wholly-owned subsidiary.

50. The new disclosures in accounts are to begin with the first
financial year *ending* six months or more *after* the passing of the
Act, which was July 27, 1967 (sec. 10(1) and sec. 57(1)(*b*)).
Accounts for all periods ending on or after January 27, 1968 will
therefore be subject to the new rules. Comparative figures for
the new items are not required in the *first* set of accounts governed
by the new Act (sec. 10(2) and (3)); the only exceptions to this
are the new requirements on directors' and top executives'
remuneration, where comparative figures *are* required right from
the start (sec. 10(5) and sec. 11(1)).

DISCLOSURE IN DIRECTORS' REPORT
MARKET VALUE OF LAND

51. If the market value of interests in land held as a fixed asset
differs substantially (whether more or less) from the balance sheet
figure and if the directors think the difference " of such significance " that the members' or debenture holders' attention should
be drawn to it, they must do so in their report (sec. 16(1)(*a*)).
This turns on a comparison of the *aggregate* market value of
land and its *aggregate* book value, not on a one-for-one comparison for each holding. " Interests in land " presumably includes buildings.

52. It is arguable that " market value " of land and buildings
here means break-up value; their going-concern value will be
reflected in the value of the earnings of the company as a whole,
and the directors could scarcely be required to draw the members'
attention to that. It seems reasonable that a difference " of such
significance " should be held to refer, not merely to size, but also

D

to usefulness. The fact that land and buildings could only be sold on a break-up basis for much less than the figure at which they stand in the accounts is of little relevance as long as the company is continuing to trade profitably and there is no intention of parting with them; *sed aliter* if the company is making losses. In ordinary circumstances it seems probable that a large unrealised surplus will be of more interest to the members than a large but hypothetical deficit. Where the " market value " is given in accordance with this provision, the basis on which it has been estimated should also be given together with the allowance, if any, that is to be made for tax and betterment levy on a disposal.

DIRECTORS' INTERESTS IN CONTRACTS

53. The present law requires a director to disclose his interest in contracts to which the company is a party to his fellow directors; the new Act requires disclosure to be made also to the members in the directors' report, if the directors consider it important enough (sec. 16(1)(c)). The section applies only to contracts with the company itself and not to those with a subsidiary, but directors might well be reluctant to take advantage of this. The section does not apply to contracts between the company and another company, where the director's *only* interest is that he is a director of that other company (sec. 16(3)). This exemption would therefore not cover cases where the director was also a significant shareholder in that other company.

54. Service contracts are excluded from the above provision (sec. 16(3)) ; a register of these, if they cover U.K. employments and have at least twelve months to run or are terminable within that period only by the company making payment, must be kept by the company for the members (and only the members) to inspect (sec. 26(1), (4) and (8)). This register also applies to service contracts with the company only, not to those with subsidiaries. A wholly-owned subsidiary's members consist only of its holding company, and as no-one has a right to inspect the subsidiary's register except its members, this could be a loop-hole. Present Stock Exchange requirements call for disclosure at the registered or transfer office of service contracts with subsidiaries (" Admission of Securities to Quotation ", June 1966, page 98).

ARRANGEMENTS TO BENEFIT DIRECTORS

55. Arrangements to which the company is a party and which are designed to benefit directors by means of their acquiring shares or debentures in *any* body corporate (including the company itself) must be disclosed by the directors (sec. 16(1)(*d*)). This is so whether or not the directors think it important, and whether or not the benefit is included in the accounts—it seems likely that it would be—as part of the total figure of directors' remuneration.

DIRECTORS' SHAREHOLDINGS

56. The directors' report must give particulars of the directors' interests in the shares and debentures of the company or other group companies at the beginning and end of the financial year (sec. 16(1)(*e*). Details must be given for each director. There are no exemptions for triviality, and nil returns *are* required. The information is to be taken from the register of directors' shareholdings, and is to include the interests of spouses and infant children. The section does not specify that the nature of the directors' interests (*e.g.* whether as beneficiary or trustee) should be quoted in the report; this is recorded in the register when the director so requires, and if it is, it should be repeated to the members. Problems on determining directors' interests in shares are discussed in Chapter III of this booklet.

SUBSTANTIALLY DIFFERING CLASSES OF BUSINESS

Where the company or group carries on two or more classes of business that in the opinion of the directors differ substantially from each other, the directors' report must describe them and give the split of turnover and profit before tax between them (sec. 17(1) and (2)). It is suggested that the "substantial difference" refers to horizontal rather than vertical integration. Different activities in the same line of business—*e.g.* manufacturing a product and selling it, would on this view not need to be split; the same activities in different lines of business—*e.g.* selling radio sets and selling ice cream—would be split. This is likely to be the more practicable view, as analysing profit to the successive stages of a vertical operation can raise almost metaphysical problems.

58. The Act does not require disclosure of the geographical spread of turnover or profit. A geographical split, however, will sometimes be a useful one to give, and is required by the Stock Exchange for quoted companies (" Admission of Securities to Quotation ", June 1966, page 96). There is no requirement to give the split of net assets corresponding to the disclosed split of turnover and profit, but plainly it must always be helpful to include this.

59. Companies that are neither holding nor subsidiary companies and whose turnover does not exceed £50,000 do not have to give the split of turnover and profits, as of course they are not required to disclose turnover at all (sec. 17(1) and para. 35 above).

60. There is no exemption for subsidiary companies, but intermediate holding companies are excused from complying with the *group* requirements if they do not prepare consolidated accounts (sec. 17(2)(a)). Separate figures are not required for banking, discounting or such other class as may be exempted by the Board of Trade from showing turnover figures in the accounts (sec. 17(1) and para. 32 above).

61. The problems of fairly allocating group or head office expenses, interest, research, publicity, management time and so on will frequently be great. It may be sufficient in many cases to show the gross contributions to profit of different activities separately, treating unallocated charges as a single deduction from the total. The results of the split, however performed, showing which activities have contributed what share of the profit or loss for the year, will have a most significant bearing on the true and fair view shown by the accounts. As this information is part of the directors' report the auditors are not asked to give their opinion on it; even so it will be impossible for them not to be concerned, if not with the mechanics of its computation, at least with its general truth and fairness. It is a matter for regret that this requirement was not made part of the accounts.

NUMBER OF EMPLOYEES AND AGGREGATE WAGES

62. The directors' report must show the average number of employees on the payroll throughout the year and their aggregate remuneration for the year (sec. 18(1)). The " average number "

is to be found by a calculation of the total employed, whether whole or part time, in each week of the financial year divided by the number of weeks (sec. 18(3)). The calculation is to be on a weekly basis whether remuneration is paid weekly or monthly. Overseas employees are excluded (sec. 18(6)).

63. The calculation includes salary earners as well as wage earners, since it covers everyone employed by the company under a contract of service (sec. 18(3)). Sub-contracted labour and gangs will therefore not be covered, nor possibly employees of partnerships formed by companies.

64. " Remuneration " is to include bonuses, whether contractual or *ex gratia* (sec. 18(4)). It does not include the estimated money value of benefits receivable otherwise than in cash (a provision requiring this was deleted from the Bill) ; such things as pension contributions, luncheon vouchers, subsidised canteens and sports clubs, company cars and accommodation should therefore be left out.

65. Where there are subsidiaries, the information has to be given on a group basis (sec. 18(2)). The group " average number " calculation can, for convenience, be the sum of the averages of all the individual companies that have been part of the group for the *full* year. Wholly-owned subsidiaries of U.K. parents do not have to give this information. Nor—a useful saving—do companies and groups that had on average less than 100 employees throughout the year (sec. 18(5)).

66. It is plain that any information given under this provision can be no more than a rough guide. It is suggested that the necessary calculations can therefore be made broadly, using estimates wherever helpful rather than detailed analyses.

POLITICAL AND CHARITABLE CONTRIBUTIONS

67. If political or charitable contributions severally or together exceed £50 the directors' report must give the total spent " on each of the purposes " (sec. 19(1)). It is thought that the phrase " each of the purposes " means two purposes in total—*i.e.* a total for charitable and a total for political, and not each of the charitable and each of the political purposes. For political contributions individually exceeding £50 the report must also

specify the recipient and the party supported; similar detail is not required of the individual charitable donations. There is an exemption for the wholly-owned subsidiaries of U.K. parents, but the directors' report of a parent company (which is not itself such a wholly-owned subsidiary) must give the above information on a group basis; this is likely to be in many cases a complex task (sec. 19(2)). Contributions to overseas charities are not required, but overseas political contributions are (sec. 19(4)).

68. The section applies where a company has " given money for . . . charitable purposes ", these being " purposes which are exclusively charitable " (sec. 19(1) and (5)). The matter is not free from doubt, but it is submitted that this wording is not apt to cover those charities that a company supports mainly for business reasons—e.g. local welfare organisations that benefit employees, or universities doing research in the company's field. Disclosure would on this view be restricted to those donations that a company makes without expecting a return.

EXPORTS

69. If the company's business " consists in, or includes, the supplying of goods ", the directors' report must state the value of goods exported from the United Kingdom during the year, or if there were none, must say so (sec. 20(1)). The concept of a business that " includes the supplying of goods " is, no doubt deliberately, vague. Arguments could be put forward to show that it covered building contractors, suppliers of know-how, providers of computer soft-ware, operators of ships and aircraft, hirers of assets; and arguments could be brought forward on the other side to say that it covered none of these things. It is suggested that the phrase should be construed restrictively to cover only those cases where supplying goods is a significant part of the total activity; otherwise the disclosures produced by the section would be absurd.

70. There is naturally nothing in the Act to prevent directors giving more information. Thus they may well wish, in the present climate of opinion, to give estimated figures of foreign currency earnings where the activity was something other than the export of goods—e.g. shipping, insurance or hotels.

71. The wording of the section appears apt to cover goods that have been transferred abroad but not sold, and U.K. sales to group companies overseas. It is not apt to cover sales of goods manufactured overseas, and U.K. sales incorporated in goods which are later exported by someone else. It does not specify whether exports are to be stated c.i.f. or f.o.b. Where the figures are material the report should make these various matters clear and, where practicable, should give additional facts in explanation. Goods exported as an agent are disregarded (sec. 20(3)).

72. The section does not apply to companies whose total turnover does not exceed £50,000 a year, whether group companies or not (sec. 20(1)). The section applies to subsidiaries, whether wholly-owned or not, and parent companies must give the information on a group basis (sec. 20(2)). The £50,000 exemption applies to a group only if (i) it presents consolidated accounts, (ii) the consolidation covers *all* subsidiaries, and (iii) the consolidated turnover disclosed in the accounts does not exceed £50,000 (sec. 20(2)). No disclosure is required if the company satisfies the Board of Trade that it would not be in the national interest (sec. 20(4)).

GENERAL

73. There are only two exemptions in the requirements on directors' reports for the wholly-owned subsidiaries of a U.K. company (employees and wages, para. 65 above, and political and charitable contributions, para. 67 above). There are three exemptions for small companies, although they are " small " in different ways (employees and wages where there are less than 100 employees, para. 65 above, and substantially differing classes of business and exports where turnover does not exceed £50,000, paras. 59 and 72 above). Otherwise, all the provisions on directors' reports apply to every company, however small, subsidiary or private.

74. Comparative figures for items shown in the directors' report are not required by the Act unless information is given there which otherwise would have had to form part of the accounts (sec. 22). It is suggested, however, that the contents will in general be much more meaningful if comparative figures are shown.

75. The new disclosures in directors' reports begin with those relating to the first financial year *ending* six months or more *after* the passing of the Act, which was July 27, 1967 (sec. 21 and sec. 57(1)(*b*)). This is the same as for the accounts requirements (para. 50 above). There is one exception: for the disclosure of the profit and turnover split between differing classes of business the starting date is six months later (sec. 57(1)(*c*)).

CHAPTER III

OTHER ASPECTS OF THE COMPANIES ACT 1967

STRUCTURE OF THE ACT

1. Before dealing with the legislation not covered in the other chapters, it is worthwhile considering the structure of the new Act.

Part I (with schedules 1 to 4) is an extension and in a few instances a modification of the Companies Act 1948 and together with that Act and the Companies (Floating Charges) (Scotland) Act 1961 it will be known as the Companies Acts 1948 to 1967.

Part II (with schedule 5 and Part I of schedule 6) provides additional legislation to the Insurance Companies Act 1958, all of which will be cited as the Insurance Companies Acts 1958 to 1967. Part II of schedule 6 amends the Industrial Assurance Act 1923.

Part III provides the Board of Trade with new powers of inspection of any company's books and papers and of entry and search of premises.

Part IV revises the law on the size of partnerships for certain professions.

Part V amends the law on moneylenders.

Part VI and the remaining schedules link this Act with other Acts, provide for consequential amendments to and repeals of earlier legislation and, for the purpose of the Protection of Depositors Act 1963, re-define " audited accounts " and " a banking or discount company ".

2. This chapter deals with the remainder of Part I not covered elsewhere and with Parts III and IV. Insurance companies and moneylenders are not covered by these comments in view of their special nature.

3. All references are to the sections of the 1967 Act.

COMPANY LAW AMENDMENTS

4. The remaining sections of Part I (apart from sections 35-42 on Inspection which are covered together with Part III starting on page 73) are dealt with under four headings:—

  A. The abolition of the exempt private company.
  B. Re-registration of companies.
  C. Additional responsibilities of the company and its directors.
  D. Miscellaneous amendments of the 1948 Act.

A. THE ABOLITION OF THE EXEMPT PRIVATE COMPANY
(sec. 2.)

5. The status of the exempt private company has been abolished. It was created by the Companies Act 1948 in an attempt to define the family business incorporated as a private company which would find the disclosure to the public of its personal affairs embarrassing. However the complex definition laid down by that Act has proved too wide and the exemption claimed by two-thirds of the 540,000 registered companies was probably never intended to apply in many cases.

6. The privileges enjoyed by an exempt private company, apart from the great advantage of not having to file accounts with the Registrar, were:—

  (a) it did not need to appoint a qualified accountant as auditor and could appoint as auditor a partner or employee of an officer of the company; and
  (b) it was free to make or guarantee loans to directors and provide security for loans made by others to directors.

7. The Jenkins Committee, in recommending the abolition of the exempt private company, found very little support for these last two advantages and considered that the filing of accounts was a necessary protection for creditors outweighing the benefits of secrecy for a small company. The new Act (sec. 2) withdraws all these privileges as from January 27, 1968. Some of the effects of this withdrawal are considered in the following paragraphs.

THE FILING OF ACCOUNTS

8. Companies which wish to keep their affairs completely private whilst retaining a corporate structure now have the option of becoming unlimited and so avoiding the requirement of filing accounts (as dealt with in more detail later in this chapter). However, shareholders should pause before they decide to risk the dangers of unlimited liability, because the Act goes a little way towards helping the small company to avoid disclosure to the public of some of the potentially more embarrassing information. In addition, the future company legislation that the Government intends to introduce could define a new type of status suitable for the small family concern.

9. To assist the small company, the Act provides that :—

(a) a company which is neither a holding company nor a subsidiary need not disclose in its accounts submitted to the members or to the Registrar:—

(i) details of turnover, as required by schedule 2, if the total in the financial year does not exceed £50,000 (sch. 2, para. 13A(5));

(ii) details of directors' emoluments under sections 6 and 7 if the total amount (calculated as for section 196(1)(a) of the 1948 Act) does not exceed £7,500 in any financial year (sec. 6(5)). However the *total amount* of the emoluments still has to be disclosed under section 196 of the 1948 Act, so that the small family business gains little from the exemption;

(b) companies or groups of companies need not disclose in their directors' report:—

(i) details of exports as required by section 20 if the total turnover as a company, or as a group of companies, does not exceed £50,000 in the financial year;

(ii) details of the average number of people employed and the aggregate paid as required by section 18, if the average number of persons employed weekly during the financial year by the company or by the group is less than 100.

10. The Jenkins Committee commented that, although exempt private companies were already under a legal obligation to prepare

annual accounts for members, the filing of accounts might secure a more regular observance of the law. Former exempt private companies which have been lax in preparing and circulating accounts may need to take early professional advice on the requirements of the Companies Acts, as the first annual return to be filed after January 26, 1968 must have accounts attached. It is not too early to begin to make arrangements for all the information required by the Acts to be available when needed, bearing in mind particularly that comparative figures will be required (except that in the financial year to which the new provisions first apply, there will be some exceptions for the information first required by the 1967 Act (sec. 10—see chapter II, paragraph 50)).

QUALIFICATION OF AUDITORS

11. The requirements for former exempt private companies regarding the qualifications of auditors are dealt with in chapter V commencing at paragraph 2.

LOANS TO DIRECTORS

12. Former exempt private companies are no longer excluded from the effect of section 190(1) of the 1948 Act, which prohibits the lending of money by a company to its own directors or those of its holding company or the guaranteeing or provision of security for a loan to such directors. This prohibition only affects future loans, and the Act neither invalidates nor requires repayment of current loans. No legislation has been introduced to prevent the making of loans to a director's family, his associates or to companies in which he is a controlling shareholder. On the other hand, directors will not normally be able to avail themselves of employees' loan facilities (*e.g.* for housing).

B. RE-REGISTRATION OF COMPANIES (sec. 43-45)

13. As we have seen, the legislature, by its abolition of the exempt private company in section 2 of the Act has adopted the principle that the privilege of limited liability should carry with it the obligation to file accounts with the Registrar of Companies. This is followed logically in section 47 by the converse principle that unlimited liability can merit the privilege of non-disclosure. The section provides that section 127 of the 1948 Act (accounts to

be annexed to the annual return) shall not apply to unlimited companies except for those which stand in the relationship of parent or subsidiary to a limited company or those which carry on the business of the promotion of trading stamp schemes within the meaning of the Trading Stamps Act 1964. For this purpose, the definition of subsidiary is extended to a company where two or more limited companies have rights which, if held by one of them, would have made that company its subsidiary.

14. Companies without limit on the liability of their members are rarely encountered at present. (In 1966 out of some 28,500 new company registrations in Great Britain, only 57 were unlimited companies). The medium was rendered necessary in principle because it formed the only way in which more than twenty people (ten in the case of banking) could associate together for business purposes without limitation of liability. The 1967 Act has rendered the preservation of the unlimited company for this particular purpose rather less meaningful since in Part IV it exempts partnerships of solicitors, accountants and members of a recognised stock exchange from any limitation on the number of partners. The Board of Trade may by regulation extend this exemption to other types of partnerships. These powers will be reserved for other professional bodies.

15. If existing limited companies think it worthwhile, they have now been given the opportunity to re-register as unlimited. Procedures for this re-registration are provided in the 1967 Act. The 1948 Act did contain machinery in section 16 for an unlimited company to re-register with limited liability, but this section was difficult to interpret and has been abolished, to be replaced by provisions somewhat similar to those now devised for the reverse change.

RE-REGISTRATION OF A LIMITED COMPANY AS UNLIMITED (sec. 43)

16. This will be carried out in the following way after October 26, 1967:—

(i) The prescribed form of application, signed by a director or the secretary, is lodged with the Registrar of Companies for either Scotland or England (dependent upon the situation of the registered office). This prescribed form, when published by the Board of Trade, should include the alterations necessary to be made to the memorandum and articles of the company so as to enable it to comply with the requirements of the 1948 Act as an unlimited company.

Accompanying the application form there must be:—

(a) A prescribed form of assent to the change of liability signed by or on behalf of all the members (again this form has not yet been published).

(b) A statutory declaration by all the directors of the company that the persons by whom or on whose behalf the form of assent is subscribed constitute the whole membership of the company. The directors are obliged to take all reasonable steps to satisfy themselves that persons subscribing to the form of assent on behalf of others are lawfully entitled to do so.

(c) A print of the memorandum of association of the company incorporating the proposed alterations.

(d) A print of the articles of association incorporating the proposed alterations and additions.

(ii) The Registrar then issues a certificate of incorporation of the company with unlimited liability. The issue automatically changes the liability status of the company and effects the alterations and additions to the memorandum and articles as if the latter had been carried out by resolution of the company. Here appears to be a departure from the hitherto accepted principle that the memorandum and articles of a company can only be altered by the members in general meeting. Unless the alterations and additions appeared in the prescribed form of assent, the memorandum and articles of the company could presumably be changed, unknown to the members under this procedure.

17. On a winding-up subsequent to the change of status, past members of the company at the time of re-registration, who do not become members again, are not to be liable to contribute more than they would have contributed had there been no re-registration.

RE-REGISTRATION OF AN UNLIMITED COMPANY AS LIMITED (sec. 44)

18. The new procedure, again after October 26, 1967, will be as follows:—

(i) The company in general meeting passes a special resolution to make the change. The resolution must:—

(a) state the manner in which the liability of the members is to be limited (i.e. by shares or guarantee) and, if the company is to have a share capital, state what that is to be; and

(b) provide for the making of such alterations to the memorandum and such alterations and additions to the articles of the company as may be appropriate for the company in its re-registered form.

(ii) The prescribed form of application for re-registration (still to be published) signed by a director or the secretary of the company is lodged with the appropriate Registrar of Companies accompanied by prints of the memorandum and articles as altered by the special resolution.

(iii) The Registrar then issues a certificate of incorporation of the company with limited liability, so automatically changing the liability status of the company. The new Act provides that the alterations and additions to the memorandum and articles take effect upon the issue of the certificate.

19. The provisions as to contribution on a subsequent winding-up are intricate and far-reaching, but this is no doubt essential since the company is not bound to consider solvency or inform its creditors before limiting its liability. The provisions are:—

(a) Present members of the company in so far as they were members at the time of re-registration are liable to contribute without limit in respect of the debts and liabilities contracted before the change. Past members of the company who were members at the time of re-registration are similarly liable if winding-up commences within three years of re-registration (amending sec. 212(1)(a) of the 1948 Act).

(*b*) If none of the members at the time of re-registration remains as a member when winding-up commences, then, notwithstanding that the existing members with limited liability may have satisfied their contributions, both present and past members at the time of re-registration can be called upon to contribute without limit, subject to the provisions outlined in the previous paragraph.

20. It is interesting to note that sections 43 and 44 appear to contemplate only one change of liability status during the life of a company. There can be no effective second thoughts after re-registration.

C. ADDITIONAL RESPONSIBILITIES OF THE COMPANY AND ITS DIRECTORS (sec. 25-32)

21. The legislation summarised under this heading appears to have two objects: firstly to expose and discourage any personal gain by a director from his inside knowledge of the company's affairs and secondly to make clear the identity of the major shareholders in a company. There are severe penalties for not complying with the law both for directors and their families.

22. At the end of this section is a summary of the immediate action which the company secretary needs to take as a result of these new provisions.

OPTION DEALINGS BY DIRECTORS (sec. 25)

23. Directors who purchase options to buy or sell the quoted shares or debentures of their own company or any companies in the same group will be guilty of an offence after October 26, 1967. The Act endorses the Jenkins Committee view that a director should not be allowed to make use of inside information about his company for personal gain. Directors, in this instance, include any person in accordance with whose directions or instructions the directors are accustomed to act unless they do so on advice given by this person in a professional capacity (sec. 56(3)). Wives and husbands of directors and their infant (or minor) children

(including adopted and step-children) are similarly covered by the prohibition (sec. 30), but officers of the company other than directors are not. The ban covers not only the quoted shares or debentures of the company but also the quoted shares or debentures of any holding, subsidiary or fellow subsidiary company. The buying of a right to subscribe for shares in or debentures of a company and the purchase of debentures carrying a subscription or conversion option are allowed. Thus the buying of options under a company's *bona fide* share option scheme is still legal.

24. The Board of Trade have taken powers under section 32 to appoint inspectors to investigate share and option dealings whenever they think a contravention of this section may have taken place. Section 167 of the 1948 Act (regarding the production of evidence by officers and agents of a company to inspectors) is specially extended to cover past and present members of a group of companies of which the company is or was a member and to apply to the members of any stock exchange and licensees and exempted dealers under the Prevention of Fraud (Investments) Act 1958. The cost of the investigation is to be defrayed by the Board of Trade, who may publish the report.

AVAILABILITY TO MEMBERS OF SERVICE CONTRACTS OF DIRECTORS (sec. 26)

25. After October 26, 1967, every company must have available to members copies of each director's current service contract with the company or, where the contract is not in writing, a memorandum setting out the terms of the contract. In any case where there is no written agreement, the statement prepared under the requirements of the Contracts of Employment Act 1963 should provide the basis for the memorandum. Exceptions to these requirements are contracts with less than twelve months to run or those which can be terminated within twelve months without compensation or those requiring a director to work wholly or mainly abroad. Surprisingly in the case of a company in a group where any of its directors have contracts of service with other companies in the group, details of these contracts do not have to be maintained by the company for the Act. (Stock Exchange

E

regulations differ—see page 70). These agreements may be inspected at " an appropriate place " (defined below), free of charge during business hours (subject to such reasonable restriction as the company in general meeting decides but not less than two hours per day). There is no right to require copies. Wholly owned subsidiaries must also provide the information on directors' service contracts for the benefit of their holding company. " An appropriate place " may be the registered office or the place where the register of members is kept or a company's principal place of business (sec. 26(2)). The Registrar must be notified of the location unless the information is always kept at the registered office.

DISCLOSURE OF DIRECTORS' INTERESTS IN COMPANIES (sec. 27-29)

26. The main effect of the complex provisions of sections 27-29 is to replace the provisions of section 195 of the 1948 Act regarding the maintenance of a register of directors' shareholdings. It is now required that all directors of a company shall (" director " being defined as for option dealings):—

> (a) declare to the company all interests in any type of share or debenture of the company or, if in a group, in companies in that group whether held by themselves or their near relatives (as defined for option dealings); and
>
> (b) disclose all changes in their interests.

Directors' interests on October 27, 1967 must be reported by November 15, 1967 and persons subsequently becoming directors must report theirs to the company within fourteen days after their appointment. After any " event " causing a subsequent change in interest, details must be reported to the company within fourteen days after the event or after the date when the director first knew of the event (Saturdays, Sundays and Bank Holidays are excluded from the fourteen days). An " event " would normally be the purchase or sale of shares or perhaps an inheritance. In section 27(1)(b) the Act covers most eventualities in a list of the " events " which must be notified.

27. The notice has to state the number of shares of each class and the amount of the debentures concerned, the date of the event and the price or consideration involved. There is no specific

requirement to state the nature of the event, but it would seem logical to do so. Greater detail must be given of dealings in options to subscribe for shares (see sec. 27(7)). In order to assist the company secretary, the notice must state the purpose for which it is prepared. Wholly-owned subsidiaries have to be informed by their own directors of their dealings in shares or debentures of other companies in the same group or in the company's own debentures.

28. Every company is required to keep a properly indexed register of the information provided by directors on behalf of themselves or their families, up-dated within three working days of receipt and with the entries for each director in chronological sequence (sec. 29). A director may have the nature and extent of any interests recorded. A company must itself record in the register any right to subscribe to any shares or debentures in the company whenever it is granted to a director and the exercising of that right whether exercised in the name of the director or not. A director assumes this obligation where rights are granted to his immediate family as defined for section 25 (sec. 30).

29. The register is to be open to any person during business hours at the company's registered office or wherever the register of members is kept. It must also be available to anyone attending the annual general meeting. Copies must be supplied within ten days of anyone's request. A summary of the interests of each director and his family at the beginning and end of the financial period has to be set out in the directors' report (sec. 16(1)(e)— see Chapter II, paragraph 56).

30. The Board of Trade have the same power to investigate directors' share dealings as they have with option dealings (sec. 32).

DEFINITION OF DIRECTOR'S INTERESTS (sec. 28)

31. Problems may arise in determining a director's interest in a share. Section 28 casts a wide net by stating (broadly) that the remoteness of the interest, the manner in which it arises, restrictions on the rights of ownership or even the fact that the shares are unidentifiable, are insufficient to exclude an interest.

32. However, it then goes on to specify certain cases in which the director is " interested " or " uninterested ". These are:—

" INTERESTED "

A beneficiary under a trust holding shares or debentures unless the trust is discretionary.

A person controlling a company which holds shares or debentures (" control " in this case means *de facto* control of the board or the entitlement to exercise one-third or more of the voting power at a general meeting).

A person with rights to call for the delivery of shares or debentures or to enforce an uncompleted contract for his purchase of them, or to exercise any holder's rights.

In the case of a joint interest, both persons are deemed to have an interest.

A trustee unless he is a simple trustee (Scotland) or a bare or custodian trustee (England and Wales), when he is deemed to be uninterested. A bare or simple trustee is one having no beneficial interest in the trust property and no active duties to perform in fulfilling his trust (*e.g.* a nominee).

" UNINTERESTED "

Remaindermen and reversioners (fiars in Scotland) under a trust during the currency of a life interest.

A proxy or a company's or shareholder's representative.

Authorised unit trust schemes and certain church funds.

The Board of Trade may exempt other types of interest from having to be notified (sec. 27(1)) and it has already been indicated that these powers will be used to eliminate interests of little or no significance.

33. No director is under any obligation until he knows of his or his family's interest but the fact that he may suddenly become aware of this interest is sufficient indication that there are likely to be considerable difficulties in operating this section in practice.

ACQUISITIONS OF INTERESTS IN QUOTED COMPANIES (sec. 33 & 34)

34. The identity of the owners of large holdings of shares carrying unrestricted voting rights in a quoted company could be common knowledge in future. Anyone (including a director) who holds or subsequently acquires an interest of 10% or more in the nominal value of the voting share capital of a quoted company must disclose the amount of his interest to the company. Thereafter all " events " (or changes in interest) must be reported to the company until after the holder's interest has fallen below 10%. Notice has to be given in writing by November 16, 1967 for interests on October 27, 1967 and within fourteen days (excluding week-ends and Bank Holidays) after subsequently acquiring shares or an " event " arising or the shareholder becoming aware of its arising.

35. The company is required to keep a properly indexed register of any interests at the place where the company's register of directors' interests is kept and on the same basis. Information supplied must be entered within three days of notification. Apart from certain information on companies incorporated or operating overseas, which the Board of Trade agree would be harmful to disclose, the details of the register must be available to anyone in business hours (business hours to be fixed by the company as in section 26) and copies may be demanded by anyone and must be sent within ten days. The companies concerned are those which have any part of their share capital quoted (whether or not it is voting capital) but the interests to be registered are those in voting capital (voting capital is that which carries the right to vote at any general meeting in all circumstances).

36. These provisions apply to non-resident shareholders but enforcement may prove difficult in practice.

37. A notice of a change in shareholding must give the name and address of the person having the interest, specifying the change, the date when it occurred and the number and type of unrestricted voting shares in which he is interested after the change. There is no requirement to notify the consideration.

38. The rules for defining an interest are the same as those for the disclosure of directors' interests except that the interests of

spouses and infant children are not relevant, and there are also to be disregarded:—

> (a) a life interest under an irrevocable settlement where the settlor has retained no interest in income and capital;
>
> (b) an interest of a person holding shares as security in the ordinary course of his business of lending money;
>
> (c) certain formal interests of the Courts; and
>
> (d) any other interests which may be prescribed for this purpose by Board of Trade regulations.

39. There are no provisions for having the nature of the interest entered in the register nor surprisingly are there any provisions covering " associated " or " connected " persons. It is thus possible for a consortium to acquire *collective* control without disclosing it. The company has no duty to notify shareholders of the contents of the register.

COMPARISON WITH STOCK EXCHANGE REQUIREMENTS

40. The memoranda of guidance and requirements of the Federation of Stock Exchanges in Great Britain and Northern Ireland for companies applying for quotations for securities differ from those of the new Act. For example, the Stock Exchange requires disclosure in or with the annual accounts of " substantial " holdings and beneficial interests in any part of the share capital, " substantial " not being defined and beneficial interests possibly not normally being within a company's knowledge. On the other hand the Act requires holdings of 10% or over in unrestricted voting shares to be recorded in a register kept by the company. Secondly directors' or their families' interests in shares through trusts are treated differently in some instances by the Stock Exchange and by the Act. Another anomaly arises in connection with the availability of a director's service contract with a subsidiary of his company. Such contracts are required to be made available for inspection prior to and during the Annual General Meeting of his company under the Stock Exchange regulations but there is no provision for shareholders of the parent company to see them under the Act.

A SUMMARY OF THE IMMEDIATE REQUIREMENTS

41. It might be helpful at this point to sum up the action that requires to be taken by the secretary of a company before October 27, 1967.

(1) Open a properly indexed register setting out the required details of directors' interests and, where relevant, those of their families in shares or debentures in the company or companies within the same group.

(2) In the case of quoted companies open a register, if necessary, setting out the required details of shareholders of 10% or more of the unrestricted voting capital.

(3) Prepare copies or, where not reduced to writing, a written memorandum, setting out the terms of service contracts of directors for inspection by members.

(4) See that directors are aware of the provisions of the new Act and in particular advise them that:—

(a) they should notify the company of their present holdings and any future changes in holdings in shares and debentures of the company (and those of their spouses and infant children) and in holdings in companies in the same group as their own company. This information is necessary for the company to set up the new register of the interests of directors and their immediate families. A form for directors to complete is probably essential; it should set out details of what constitutes an " interest ". A procedure for notifying changes in interests should be set up underlining the importance of immediate notification;

(b) action has been taken under (2) and/or (3) above;

(c) purchases of options by them or their spouses and infant children in the quoted shares or debentures of the company or of companies in the same group carry severe legal penalties except when the options are granted by the company;

(d) they, together with other officers of the company, have obligations under penal provisions to make the necessary returns and entries in the registers.

(5) Set up arrangements for the maintenance and inspection of registers and directors' contracts as required under the Act.

(6) Ensure that subsidiary companies and their directors are fully informed of the legislation particularly with regard to option and share dealings in the shares of the companies in their group.

(7) Notify the Registrar of Companies of the place where the information regarding directors' contracts of service and the registers of directors' interests and of large shareholders are kept if not at the registered office of the company.

D. MISCELLANEOUS AMENDMENTS OF THE 1948 ACT

42. Some minor sections of the new Act which are of general interest are:—

CHANGE OF NAME (sec. 46)

43. The Board of Trade can now direct a company to change its name if in the opinion of the Board it gives so misleading an indication of the nature of its activities as to cause harm to the public. The company may appeal to the Court within three weeks of the direction.

FEES (sec. 48)

44. The opportunity has been taken of increasing the fees payable to the Registrar and of providing for future amendments to the scale of fees by Government regulation. The new fees payable after October 26, 1967, are set out in schedule 3 (reproduced on pages 32 and 33). After that date the fee for filing the annual return is £3 and for changing a company's name £10.

COPIES TO REGISTRAR (sec. 51)

45. Copies of resolutions and agreements need no longer be printed before submitting them to the Registrar. Other forms of reproduction may be used if approved by the Registrar.

COPIES OF REGISTERS (sec. 52)

46. An increase has been approved in the maximum charge for copies of the registers of share or debenture holdings (2s. per 100 words) or the debenture trust deed (4s. for a copy or where not printed 2s. per 100 words).

POWERS OF INVESTIGATION BY
THE BOARD OF TRADE (PART III)

47. The growing number of serious company insolvencies in recent years has given rise to increased public demand for the Board of Trade to have wider powers of inspection. The 1948 Act appeared to give the Board reasonable grounds to appoint an inspector to enquire into the affairs of a company, but the very fact that the appointment cast a stigma on the company made the Board reluctant to act unless it had very strong reasons for doing so. The Jenkins Committee suggested that the way round this dilemma was to give the Board power to obtain documents and information from companies with a view to deciding whether or not to appoint an inspector. The new Act adopts this suggestion, giving the Board of Trade authority to call for evidence whenever they think there is good reason to do so. Presumably they will do this without public announcement. The Act then goes on to sharpen the teeth already given the Board by the 1948 Act and by the Protection of Depositors Act 1963. It will be interesting to see in what circumstances it subsequently appears that the Board made use of their new powers.

INSPECTION OF COMPANIES' BOOKS AND
PAPERS (sec. 109-118)

48. Under Part III of the new Act (which does not apply to Northern Ireland) the Board of Trade may require at any time any company (as defined by section 109) to produce to them any books or papers of the company that the Board may specify *if they think there is good reason to do so* (sec. 109). The Board may:—

(a) demand the production of books or papers of the company or, if not produced, information as to where they are;

(b) obtain a search warrant to enable the police to trace books or papers (sec. 110);

(c) take copies of or extracts from books and documents; and

(d) require explanations of such books or papers from any past or present officer or employee of the company or from the person producing them. With the intention of speeding up the various stages of an investigation into a company, it has also been provided that any statements may be used in evidence against those making them.

49. Part III of the Act does not apply to privileged documents between solicitors and their clients, nor may the Board of Trade require bankers to produce documents relating to their customers' affairs unless the bank is under investigation or the customer has, under section 109, been asked to produce the document in question (sec. 116).

50. There are penalties for destroying evidence with the intent of concealing the state of affairs of the company (sec. 113) or for making false statements (sec. 114). On the other hand, those companies which supply evidence on which the Board find no grounds for further action are protected in the Act against disclosure of the information to anyone except the Board or an inspector (sec. 111).

POSSIBLE ACTION BY THE BOARD OF TRADE

51. The Board of Trade may thus obtain information through their new power under Part III or under sections 18 and 19 of the Protection of Depositors Act 1963, which enables them to take action. They may also appoint an inspector in certain circumstances if further clarification is required (1948 Act, sec. 165). Armed with this evidence the Board may:—

(a) at their own cost, bring civil proceedings in the name of any company if it appears to them that it is in the public interest (sec. 37 modifying sec. 169(4) of the 1948 Act); or

(b) if the company is liable to be wound up, the Board may present the petition if it appears to them to be expedient in the public interest (sec. 35 modifying sec. 169(3)). In other cases, they may proceed under section 210 of the 1948 Act to abate any oppressive action against the minority.

52. The first two sub-sections of section 169 of the 1948 Act concerning cases of criminal liability being referred to the Lord Advocate (or Director of Public Prosecutions) have been repealed

(sec. 36). Further amendments have also been made to the 1948 Act provisions:—

  (a) giving the Board power to appoint inspectors not only where there are circumstances suggesting that the company is being run fraudulently but also in cases where it seems that there has been fraudulent trading in the past. Also these powers can now be exercised if the company is being wound up (sec. 38);

  (b) enabling inspectors to call the officers or agents of the company as witnesses (sec. 39);

  (c) giving an inspector the opportunity of informing the Board of Trade of any possible offence coming to his notice *during* his investigation so that the Board may act quickly (sec. 41); and

  (d) bringing foreign companies in business in this country on to an equal footing with U.K. registered companies (sec. 42).

53. The rarely used sections 164 and 165(a) of the 1948 Act are retained so that the Board may appoint an inspector on the application of the prescribed number of shareholders or must appoint one upon special resolution by the company or an order by the Court.

PARTNERSHIPS (PART IV)

54. The limitation upon the size of the membership of an unincorporated business association now found in section 434 of the 1948 Act dates from the Companies Act 1862 and was intended to prevent the difficulties which had been experienced by the public in dealing with large trading associations with a fluctuating membership. The result of the limitation was to compel business associations with numbers in excess of the statutory limit to organise themselves as corporations subject to statutory control. Some professions have found this limitation irritating in practice and in their case the law has been amended to allow larger partnerships.

55. Under this part of the new Act (which does not extend to Northern Ireland):—

    (*a*) banking partnerships may have a maximum of twenty members against ten previously (sec. 119); and

    (*b*) unlimited membership is available to partnerships of solicitors, accountants (recognised or authorised by the Board of Trade), members of a recognised stock exchange or to other bodies which may be specified by the Board of Trade (sec. 120).

56. The little-used Limited Partnerships Act 1907 is similarly modified by section 121 as regards partnerships of solicitors, accountants and stockbrokers but not bankers.

CHAPTER IV

TAXATION AND ESTATE DUTY PROBLEMS ARISING ON CONSIDERATION OF THE COMPANIES ACT 1967

1. The Companies Act 1967 does not itself directly affect the taxation or estate duty liabilities of companies or their shareholders. It may, however, give a fresh impetus to the reconsideration of company status which has been going on since the introduction of the changes in the system of company taxation brought about by the Finance Act 1965 and later Finance Acts. To some extent, companies may infer that they are invited to consider some change in status by virtue of the increased facilities in sections 43 and 44 respectively of the Companies Act 1967, whereby limited companies may re-register as unlimited companies and *vice versa*. Any decision to change the status of a company in this way or to cease to be a body corporate altogether will no doubt be reached only after a full appraisal of all relevant factors, including the acquisition or retention of the protection which limited liability affords, but inevitably the tax position will also have to be considered.

The purpose of the present notes is (1) to indicate the general tax position of unlimited companies, which hitherto have been a relatively uncommon form of body corporate, (2) to discuss some aspects of the taxation of partnerships and sole traders as compared with company taxation, and (3) to draw to attention several important taxation consequences arising in company liquidations.

UNLIMITED COMPANIES

2. The taxation and estate duty position of unlimited companies and their shareholders is similar to that of limited companies. Most Income Tax and Finance Acts refer to " bodies corporate," and this term includes both limited and unlimited companies.

LIABILITY FOR CORPORATION TAX ON PROFITS AND GAINS AND FOR SCHEDULE F INCOME TAX ON DISTRIBUTIONS TO MEMBERS

3. All bodies corporate, whether limited or unlimited, are liable to corporation tax on their profits and gains by virtue of section 46 of the Finance Act 1965 and are liable to account for income tax on distributions by section 47 and schedule 11 of that Act.

CLOSE COMPANY LEGISLATION

4. This also applies to unlimited companies, which, more often than not, are close companies since the share capital of an unlimited company is not easily marketable and tends therefore to be held within a family or other small group of shareholders. The ordinary shortfall rules and surtax direction procedures apply—section 77 and 78 and schedule 18 of the Finance Act 1965.

THE VALUATION OF SHARES IN UNLIMITED COMPANIES FOR ESTATE DUTY PURPOSES

5. Shares in unlimited companies are valued in much the same way as the shares of limited companies. This is especially true of large blocks of shares where a net assets basis of valuation applies, although in appropriate cases some account may be taken of the risks involved in carrying unlimited liability, thus reducing the valuation. Where a small block of shares is involved, a lower value is usually accepted compared with shares in limited companies, because of the additional risk which the minority shareholders in unlimited companies run, bearing in mind that their interest in the company's assets is limited, while their interest in the company's liabilities is not.

PARTNERSHIPS AND SOLE TRADERS

6. If a company wishes to give up its corporate status, the members continuing in business as individual proprietors or partners, the general effect is that the scheme of company taxation will no longer apply to that business and its profits and capital gains will thereafter be taxed at the rates appropriate to individuals. Subject to the special tax problems which arise on the precedent winding up of the company, the chief difficulty is to establish the relevant tax rates for comparison.

RATES OF TAX ON PROFITS

7. The question is often posed as to whether partnerships (or sole traders) pay higher or lower rates of tax than companies. This is a question that can only be answered by working out the result for each individual case both in the short term and the long term. There is no shortcut method of computation or formula which is universally applicable in all circumstances. In the case of small businesses, defined for this particular purpose as those businesses earning up to £4,000 per full-time working proprietor, there is usually very little in it, since, if desired, a company's profits up to this level can be converted to personal income of the working proprietors by way of remuneration without any serious (close company) penalty. Even where profits are higher than this, company taxation and partnership taxation may not differ materially and there is a possibility that in some cases, even with all the disadvantages of a close company, the company tax may be lighter. Where the profits are substantial, say £10,000 per annum or more per working proprietor, it is probable that a company will pay less tax than a firm or a sole trader provided it requires to retain profits for development of its business. The crucial factors are the allowance for directors' remuneration and the " shortfall " position.

One further point to bear in mind in regard to companies is that where profits are retained consistently over a period there are almost certain to be capital gains tax repercussions at some stage, *i.e.* when members dispose of their shares.

TAX ON CAPITAL GAINS

8. Individuals and firms pay tax on long-term capital gains at 30% compared with the 40%, the present rate of corporation tax, payable by companies. Individuals (including partners) may also claim to have their long-term gains taxed by the alternative method (sec. 21, F.A. 1965) which reduces the effective capital gains tax rate to not more than 20·625% where the gain (or the individual's share of it) does not exceed £5,000 and he is liable only to standard rate income tax (or less) and not to surtax. In many cases, therefore, individuals pay only half the rate of capital gains tax payable by companies. With the latter there is the further disadvantage that a double charge often arises when

shareholders realise a gain on their shares which is attributable to gains made within the company and in respect of which the company has already paid gains tax.

In the case of short-term gains, however, a company may bear less tax than an individual, as the latter is charged under Case VII at full income tax and (where appropriate) surtax rates, whereas a company pays the same rate as it does on its long-term gains.

PENSION SCHEMES

9. These are available if the business is carried on by a partnership, except that partners would not be allowed to participate in the firm's pension scheme. They would, however, be entitled to provide for retirement in other ways, for example by taking out retirement annuities under Part III of the Finance Act 1956. Where a company is converted to a partnership it is often found that a director turned partner loses something in the exchange where he has valuable pension rights. The possible loss of such benefits could well be the deciding factor in determining to continue with a company structure for the business.

WINDING UP

10. The liquidation of a company brings special tax problems. Many of these problems are problems of detail or may arise from special circumstances. The following are perhaps the more important general tax points which arise and which should be considered prior to the winding up.

AMOUNTS DISBURSED BY THE LIQUIDATOR— CAPITAL OR INCOME

11. Sums disbursed in the course of a liquidation to members are capital, provided of course that they are in respect of share capital. Any excess over the nominal value is not to be regarded as income (sec. 47(5) F.A. 1965). The member will, however, be liable to capital gains tax on any profit he makes.

CLOSE COMPANIES

12. Special rules apply to the computation of shortfall in the final accounting periods (sch. 18, paras. 12 and 13, F.A. 1965). Some care is desirable in selecting the date of liquidation.

THE TAX POSITION OF INCOME ARISING IN THE COURSE OF A LIQUIDATION

13. The liquidator is liable for tax (*i.e.* corporation tax) on such income in the usual way. In the case of close companies the income may be the subject of a surtax direction.

CAPITAL GAINS TAX

14. The liquidator is liable for capital gains tax on all realisations of assets. Members are also liable on gains arising on the disposal of their shares which takes place on liquidation.

Liquidation is not likely to affect the matter of retirement relief, and indeed the winding up process may be harmonised with an appropriate retirement to minimise not only the capital gains tax liability but also estate duty and the expense involved in the handing over of a business to a successor or heir.

OTHER TAX MATTERS

15. It has been suggested that the anti-avoidance provisions of section 28 of the Finance Act 1960 might be applied by the Inland Revenue in respect of reserves, otherwise distributable by way of dividend, released in a liquidation to shareholders. The only safe way to deal with this problem is to obtain a clearance under sub-section (10) of section 28 prior to liquidation taking place.

16. Re-registration of company status, whether from a limited to an unlimited company or *vice versa*, should not attract the tax consequences inherent in a liquidation where there is no change in the capital structure and no benefit passes to the shareholders. Companies are advised, however, to confirm this in each case with the Inland Revenue pending the issue of a practice note by that body or until a special provision of a Finance Act specifically provides that this is so. Where, however, there is a reduction or reorganisation of share capital on re-registration, some at least of the tax consequences of liquidation might ensue and care should be taken to obtain appropriate advice and Revenue clearances in such cases.

F

17. The treatment of tax losses is not affected by re-registration and, because there is no real change in the identity of the company, the unrelieved losses remain available for set off against future profits. This position remains unaltered even if the view is maintained that there has been a change of identity for tax purposes since in that event section 17 (F.A. 1954) would operate to produce the same result.

SUMMARY

18. The above notes are not, of course, exhaustive and reference should be made to the relevant Finance Acts and the principal textbooks on taxation before action is taken to change a company's status. It is hoped, however, that the general advice outlined above will be of assistance, if only to alert company advisers in regard to some of the more important taxation consequences of proposed fundamental changes in a company's structure if such a change is otherwise considered appropriate.

19. As regards the three main topics covered it may be said in conclusion that—(1) the taxation of unlimited companies and their shareholders is similar to that for limited companies; (2) the comparative taxation of partnerships and sole traders is a matter for individual consideration in accordance with the circumstances of each case; and (3) in connection with re-registration involving liquidation or otherwise it is best to be safe and to apply for clearance from the Revenue against the risk of incurring additional, possibly unquantifiable, taxation liabilities unless the company is completely satisfied by virtue of published Revenue statements or later tax legislation that no such liabilities will arise.

CHAPTER V

THE QUALIFICATIONS, APPOINTMENT, DUTIES AND RESPONSIBILITIES OF AUDITORS UNDER THE COMPANIES ACT 1967

1. The Companies Act 1967, as nineteen years ago did its immediate predecessor, brings about a considerable extension in the duties and responsibilities of the auditors of companies. In addition, it subjects the auditor to new legislation as to his eligibility to hold office. This chapter is an endeavour to outline some of the principal changes in law to which the auditor may wish to, or perhaps should, direct his attention and is also designed to provide some guidance to companies both as regards the appointment of an auditor and as to matters which for the first time are specifically subject to audit.

QUALIFICATIONS AND APPOINTMENT

2. The demise of the exempt private company has led to the changes to which effect is given in section 13, and it is interesting to note that whereas the description of the corresponding section 161 of the 1948 Act was " disqualifications for appointment as auditor " the new Act adopts the positive approach in its " qualification for appointment as auditor ". The effect of these changes is not as sweeping as had earlier been envisaged, particularly in that the auditor of a former exempt private company (who is otherwise disqualified under section 161(1) of the 1948 Act) may continue to hold office provided that he has obtained authority from the Board of Trade to be so appointed and (a) has practised as a self employed accountant throughout the twelve months ended November 3, 1966, and (b) on such date was the duly appointed auditor of a company that was then an exempt private company; he may not, however, continue to hold office in the event of any of the company's (or of its parent company's) shares or debentures being quoted on a stock exchange in Great Britain or elsewhere. Notwithstanding these provisions, eighteen months' grace,

following the coming into force of the 1967 Act, is given by which any auditor of a former exempt private company shall continue for that period to be qualified provided (i) that he is not disqualified for appointment in terms of the 1948 Act, and (ii) that none of the company's (or its parent's) shares or debentures is quoted on a stock exchange.

3. The basic condition of eligibility for appointment as auditor is still that as set out in section 161(1) of the 1948 Act, namely that to be qualified (other than in the case of the above mentioned exception) a person must be (a) a member of a body of accountants established in the United Kingdom and recognised for this purpose by the Board of Trade, or (b) one who is otherwise authorised for this purpose by the Board of Trade (i) as holding similar overseas qualifications or (ii) as having obtained adequate knowledge and experience in the course of his employment by a member of a recognised United Kingdom accountancy body. No longer, however, will a person be qualified for appointment solely by reason of his having been in practice in the United Kingdom before August 6, 1947; such a person, to remain qualified, must have made application to the Board of Trade before the date upon which sub-section (4) of section 13 of the 1967 Act comes into force, namely January 27, 1968. At present the United Kingdom bodies recognised by the Board of Trade under section 161(1) of the 1948 Act are:—

(a) The Institute of Chartered Accountants in England and Wales;
(b) The Institute of Chartered Accountants of Scotland;
(c) The Institute of Chartered Accountants in Ireland; and
(d) The Association of Certified and Corporate Accountants.

The provision contained in section 159(2) of the 1948 Act whereby, except in the circumstances there stated, a retiring auditor shall be reappointed without a resolution being passed to that effect at an annual general meeting, continues to operate.

4. The change that may most affect practising accountants is that consequential to the above-mentioned demise of the exempt private company. The auditor of such a company could be, and sometimes was, a partner or an employee of a director or secretary

(or other officer or servant) of the company, but he is no longer qualified so to act; he is, however, by concession allowed under section 13(3) of the 1967 Act to continue in office as auditor for three years and six months after the passing of the Act, with the same proviso in regard to quotation of shares or debentures as above. For this reason changes in the ranks of auditors, directors and secretaries will undoubtedly become commonplace over the next three and one-half years. Many accountants who not only act professionally in an administrative or advisory capacity for formerly exempt private companies, but whose partners act individually as secretary (or director), and who also fill the office of auditor, may find a solution in resigning the office of secretary (or director) as such and in continuing to act in an administrative or a financial advisory capacity, and also to hold the office of auditor—provided that they do not in any way become " servants " of the company. It will be interesting to follow the means by which these relationships will, effectively, continue. Companies will certainly not wish to be burdened with the probable administrative inconvenience and additional expense of employing two firms of accountants to do the jobs that one does at present.

AUDITOR'S REPORT

5. The changes brought about by section 14 of the new Act are not really so drastic in their effect as may seem from a cursory comparison of that section with section 162 and schedule 9 of the 1948 Act. The purpose of the amendment would seem to be simplification in reporting rather than alteration in principle of the auditor's basic duties as laid down by statute; these still provide in respect of him that:—

  (a) he shall report to the members on every balance sheet and profit and loss account and all group accounts laid before the company in general meeting,
  (b) his report shall be read before the company in general meeting and shall be open to inspection by any member,
  (c) he shall have a right of access at all times to the books, accounts and vouchers and to require from the company's officers such information and explanations as he deems necessary,

(*d*) he shall be entitled to attend and speak at general meetings of companies and to receive notices, etc., relative thereto, and, perhaps most important,

(*e*) his duty is to confirm, or otherwise, to the members that:—

    (i) proper books of account have been kept (and proper returns have been received from branches not visited),

    (ii) the accounts are in agreement with the books,

    (iii) the accounts have been properly prepared in accordance with the provisions of the (1948 and 1967) Companies Acts,

    (iv) the balance sheet (and consolidated balance sheet) and profit and loss account (and/or consolidated profit and loss account) give a true and fair view of the company's (group's) state of affairs and profit or loss.

6. Whereas the auditor, under the 1948 Act, had laid upon him the duty of specifically reporting on all the matters paraphrased in (*e*) above, he now is required only to report positively on (*e*) (iii) and (iv) unless he is unable to do so in the affirmative as to (i) and (ii), in which event he shall report accordingly. Furthermore, while the 1948 Act required that the auditor " report on " all these above items, the new Act alters its accent so that in regard to (i) and (ii) it is provided that it shall be " the duty of the auditor " to " carry out such investigations as will enable him to form an opinion " as to the matters there outlined. Broadly, therefore, the main effect of these provisions is firstly to legalise the now relatively familiar " shortened docquet ", and secondly to define in general terms for the auditor what he must do before he can report on accounts. It remains to be seen whether the Courts will look upon the latter as helpful in considering matters of alleged negligence which may come before them.

7. The 1948 Act (sec. 196) required auditors to include in their report details of directors' remuneration insofar as such was not disclosed in the accounts. Similarly the provisions of the 1967 Act (secs. 6, 7 and 8) include like requirements, extended to the more detailed particulars now demanded in respect of directors' and certain other employees' remuneration and waiver of directors'

emoluments (except that the details in respect of directors' remuneration need not be given where the total does not exceed £7,500 for the year under review). Here, therefore, a further duty is placed upon the auditor's shoulders; so far as directors are concerned he must see to it that the required information as to chairman's emoluments, emolument *tranches* and waivers is correct, and as to other employees (other than as excluded by subsection (1)(*b*) of section 8) he must ascertain by reference to the company's records and to information in relation to subsidiaries that total emoluments of such persons are correctly recorded in the accounts. Clearly the latter requirement will place upon (particularly) a parent company's auditor the task of ascertaining sufficient (and possibly very extensive) detail of salaries and benefits (which for this purpose exclude contributions to pension schemes) paid within a group to, or for the benefit of, all the employees of the company whose total emoluments may possibly fall within the scope of the section.

8. An unqualified report on the accounts of a company not having subsidaries might read thus:—

> "In my opinion the foregoing (or annexed, etc.) accounts (or balance sheet and profit and loss account) and notes thereon have been properly prepared in accordance with the provisions of the Companies Acts 1948 and 1967 and give (respectively) a true and fair view of the state of affairs of ABC Ltd. as at (date) and of the profit (loss) for the year ended on that date."

NEW DISCLOSURE POINTS

9. Elsewhere in this booklet there have been set out and discussed the new disclosure requirements of the 1967 Act. Insofar as these are required to be included in, or annexed to, the accounts they clearly become of prime importance to the auditor. Mention has already been made in paragraph 7 of what would appear to be the principal such matters insofar as they impinge directly upon the auditor's report itself. But as to the carrying out of the audit of the accounts much ground will also require to be covered more critically, perhaps, than heretofore.

10. In particular, for example, whereas the audit of turnover of a company has in the past been conducted with an eye to forming a view as to whether proper account has been taken of all sales transactions during a year, now the exact figure of such must be disclosed in the audited accounts—and that on a basis which is to be defined. It seems hardly necessary to elaborate on the difference in accent on this aspect of the auditor's responsibility occasioned by the new requirement. The detailed information in regard to directors' remuneration has already been touched on; auditors must, however, also satisfy themselves (in terms of section 7) as to the quantum of remuneration waived by directors. Detailed information in regard to interest charges and plant hire is now part of the accounts; the auditor will therefore cover these types of expense, often in a necessarily more exact manner than before. While he has always doubtless been fully aware of the reasons for abnormalities in the charge for taxation, he must now see to it that (where special circumstances obtain) all the relevant facts are given on the face of the accounts. None of the additional duties outlined in this paragraph should prove particularly onerous other than in terms of expenditure of additional time.

11. The new balance sheet requirements are also, in the main, more time consuming than complex. The requirement as to details of fixed asset movements has been anticipated by very many companies already; in the numerous cases, however, where this has not occurred the auditor will clearly find himself with, again, a need for extended precision. The examination of the valuation figures in respect of fixed assets, which now require to be disclosed in terms of paragraph 11(6A) of schedule 2, may be a relatively weighty task, particularly so, perhaps, in relation to the statements as to bases of valuation. In two cases considerable food for thought on the auditor's part is provided by the Act. First of all, the requirement that background information is to be given in regard to unquoted equity investments (identity in certain cases—sec. 4; financial information when shares are not valued by the directors—sch. 2, para. 5A) brings the auditor into a new field. He must, it would appear, make himself much more conversant with companies' investments than has (strictly) been the case until now. He must now measure the holdings therein

in nominal value against the appropriate capital of the company in question and the balance sheet value thereof against the total assets of the owning (*i.e.* client) company; he must also consider either (i) the basis and reliability of any valuations placed thereon by directors, or (ii) the financial information, derived from (audited) accounts of such companies, otherwise demanded, particularly, by paragraph 5A(*b*) and (*c*) of schedule 2. The former requirement (i), being the " let-out " from the provision requiring disclosure of background financial information, may well become a particularly thorny audit problem especially if the auditor either finds himself at variance with the directors on the question of approach to the valuation or feels unsure as to the directors' ability to value unquoted investments. The latter—(ii)—, while obviously involving the necessity of obtaining for examination the audited accounts of the concern(s) forming the investment(s) in question, might in certain cases place the auditor in the position of including some degree of disclaimer in his report—always assuming that he is not also the auditor of the company or companies in question. The other case is that of stock valuation where the new Act requires a statement of the basis adopted. In the common instance it is very tempting to be satisfied with a descriptive phrase such as " at the lower of cost and net realisable value ". Auditors may well find themselves looking for greater precision in terminology; is " cost " a meaningful word, particularly in relation to processed goods ?

12. The 1967 Act includes such phrases as " if material " and " where practicable ". The auditor must be clear in his mind in each case coming before him as to the degrees of materiality and practicability which he will be prepared to accept as falling into, or out of, such categories. He may also find himself in difficulties as a result of the new rulings in sections 3(1) and 16(1) whereby in the former details of holdings in subsidiaries fall to be stated in the accounts, whereas the latter involves disclosure in the directors' report of, *inter alia*, activities of (the company and) subsidiaries and any significant changes therein and in fixed assets thereof; the two statements together must make sense, but the auditor only has responsibility for the first. Section 5 imposes the requirement to disclose the identity of the company " regarded by the directors as being the company's ultimate hold-

ing company ". It seems uncertain whether the auditor has a duty to bring this matter within the scope of his report on the accounts; but if he has, an audit problem is thereby created in that it would appear doubtful whether the directors' view may be unreservedly accepted—and further enquiry might be required on the part of the auditor.

DIRECTORS' REPORT

13. The auditor is not required by the 1967 (or for that matter the 1948) Act to report on matters contained in the directors' report issued to the members of a company other than to the extent that information normally required to be disclosed in accounts is (in terms of sec. 163 of the 1948 Act) so contained. It would appear, however, that the scope of the auditor's responsibility may not be quite so easily defined as the strict terms of the statute might indicate.

14. The 1967 Act requires the disclosure in the directors' report of a number of financial facts which do not also appear in the accounts. These mainly concern attribution of turnover to, and profitability of, various classes of business, political and charitable contributions, export sales, employee and wages statistics and—in some cases—market value of land. Certain of these items may well not normally cause the auditor much worry. But insofar as the first-mentioned is concerned, the requirement is so fundamental to an appreciation of results that the correctness of the figures given must be undoubted; also the figures involved are more than ordinarily susceptible to accounting error and to opinion as to, e.g. cost allocation between activities, that a misleading picture could quite possibly be given innocently, or otherwise. Further, in regard to disclosure of market value of land if substantially different from book value, the auditor will possibly wish to ensure that the figures used are in context and not liable to mislead.

15. The auditor may well take the view that he cannot isolate his responsibility to the accounts but will wish to be satisfied that not only do the accounts which he certifies give a true and fair view of the profit and state of affairs, but that they also do so

within the context in which they are submitted to shareholders. Practice in years to come will determine the professional approach to this problem, but in the meantime it seems wise for the auditor to satisfy himself that misleading or inaccurate financial information is not contained in a directors' report. If he is dissatisfied to a material extent he would presumably suggest to his client any amendment which he considers desirable; if he fails in that approach he may wish to draw attention in his report to the fact that he takes no responsibility for the financial contents of the directors' report.

SUMMARY

16. In conclusion it might be said that from an auditor's point of view:—

- (a) in most cases he will continue to be eligible for appointment,
- (b) if his partner (or employee) acts as an officer of his client company, one of them will require to demit office within three years and six months from July 27, 1967,
- (c) his report will usually be shorter and more easily understood,
- (d) his audit scope will be increased in view of the new disclosure requirements; and he will require to apply particularly weighty consideration to a number of matters, notably in regard to unquoted investments, basis of stock valuation and basis of turnover ascertainment,
- (e) he may well, although not required to do so, find himself considering the reliability of financial contents of the directors' report.

From the company's standpoint the disclosure (and therefore also audit—so far as the accounts are concerned) provisions of the new Act will often demand a higher level of precision in recording information which will now form part of the statutory accounts. Almost certainly—except in the cases where there already is effective compliance with the 1967 Act—a higher level of audit cost to companies will arise as a result of the greater volume of work which will unavoidably be carried out by auditors in fulfilling the responsibilities placed upon them by the extensive additions to required disclosures.

17. This summary, and indeed the whole contents of this chapter, are designed to shed a little preliminary light on the type of problem likely to be faced under the new Act. Practice in the years to come will develop along lines which will become clear as time goes on; but time waits for no man and in the immediate future every auditor will find it necessary to decide upon, at least, his initial approach to the new responsibilities placed upon him.

INDEX

SHOWING PAGE NUMBERS

TRADING STAMP ACT 1964, 21, 28, 61

TURNOVER
 Directors' report, disclosure in, 21, 23, 31, 51, 52, 56, 59
 Exports, from, 21, 23, 54, 55, 59
 Profit and loss account, disclosure in, 18, 20, 42 43, 49, 59

UNLIMITED COMPANY, 21, 27, 28, 31, 34, 59, 60, 61, 62, 63, 77, 78, 81, 82

VALUERS, 13, 35

WINDING UP, CONTRIBUTIONS IN, 62, 63, 64

WORK IN PROGRESS, 14, 39, 40

Printed by William Blackwood & Sons Ltd., Edinburgh.